Brain-Compatible Activities for Mathematics

Grades K-1

Brain-Compatible Activities for Mathematics

Grades K-1

David A. Sousa

CORWIN
A SAGE Company

Copyright © 2010 by David A. Sousa

All rights reserved. When forms and sample documents are included, their use is authorized only by educators, local school sites, and/or noncommercial or nonprofit entities that have purchased the book. Except for that usage, no part of this book may be reproduced or utilized in any form or by any means, electronic or mechanical, including photocopying, recording, or by any information storage and retrieval system, without permission in writing from the publisher.

For information:

Corwin
A SAGE Company
2455 Teller Road
Thousand Oaks, California 91320
(800) 233-9936
Fax: (800) 417-2466
www.corwinpress.com

SAGE India Pvt. Ltd.
B 1/I 1 Mohan Cooperative
  Industrial Area
Mathura Road, New Delhi 110 044
India

SAGE Ltd.
1 Oliver's Yard
55 City Road
London EC1Y 1SP
United Kingdom

SAGE Asia-Pacific Pte. Ltd.
33 Pekin Street #02-01
Far East Square
Singapore 048763

Printed in the United States of America.

Library of Congress Cataloging-in-Publication Data

Sousa, David A.
Brain-compatible activities for mathematics, Grades K-1 / David A. Sousa.
    p. cm.
Includes bibliographical references and index.
ISBN 978-1-4129-6783-9 (pbk.)
    1. Mathematics—Study and teaching (Preschool)—Activity programs.
   2. Mathematics—Study and teaching (Primary)—Activity programs. I. Title.

QA135.6.S5664 2010
372.7—dc22   2009031870

This book is printed on acid-free paper.

09   10   11   12   13   10 9 8 7 6 5 4 3 2 1

Managing Editor:	Cathy Hernandez
Executive Editor:	Kathleen Hex
Editorial Assistant:	Sarah Bartlett
Developmental Writers:	Carla Hamaguchi and Karen Trayser
Developmental Editor:	Jeanine Manfro
Production Editor:	Cassandra Margaret Seibel
Copy Editor:	Barbara Corrigan
Typesetter:	C&M Digitals (P) Ltd.
Proofreader:	Kevin Gleason
Cover Designer:	Karine Hovsepian
Illustrators:	Mark Mason, Ann Iosa, Ben Mahan, Jamie Smith, Mary Rojas, Mike Wesley, Jane Yamada

Contents

Introduction

Brain-compatible math activities are fun and exciting! These activities are often hands on and involve partners, group work, and class movement, which many students enjoy. Students frequently say that mathematics is difficult for them. Therefore, as an educator, it is your job to choose materials that are likely to be effective in light of current research about how the brain learns mathematics. This book is filled with activities that are centered on brain research and that are structured to maximize the brain's learning potential.

The activities in this book are designed using a brain-compatible lesson plan format. There are nine components of the plan, but not all nine are necessary for every lesson. Those components that are most relevant to the learning objective should be emphasized:

1. anticipatory set,

2. learning objective,

3. purpose,

4. input,

5. modeling,

6. checking for understanding,

7. guided practice,

8. closure, and

9. independent practice.

Each of the components is described in detail in the book titled *How the Brain Learns Mathematics.* Refer to this book for more brain-compatible math research and other teaching strategies. When using the activities in this book, read through the activity first. Then begin preparations for the lesson. It is best to follow the lesson plan format to ensure maximum learning potential. However, meeting the needs of each student in your classroom is always first and foremost. Be flexible to ensure that all students are learning. Last, have fun! These activities may force you to step out of your comfort zone. Embrace the change, and watch your students' brains at work.

PUT IT INTO PRACTICE

How the brain learns is a fascinating and complex process. Advancements in research and technology are helping us understand specifically how the brain learns math and deals with numbers and mathematical relationships. These remarkable findings are improving teaching and learning dramatically. An educator's understanding and applying instructional approaches that are compatible with what cognitive studies tell us will only aid in his or her classroom success.

Some of the recent research discoveries about the brain can and should affect teaching and learning. For example, research tells us that

- creating and using conceptual subitizing patterns help young students develop the abstract number and arithmetic strategies they will need to master counting;
- just as phonemic awareness is a prerequisite to learning phonics and becoming a successful reader, developing number sense is a prerequisite for succeeding in mathematics;
- information is most likely to store if it makes sense and has meaning;
- too often, mathematics instruction focuses on skills, knowledge, and performance but spends little time on reasoning and deep understanding; and
- mathematics can be defined simply as the science of patterns.

A much fuller explanation of these discoveries and their implications for school and the classroom can be found in my book *How the Brain Learns Mathematics*, published by Corwin. This book is designed as a classroom resource to accompany that text. The activities in this book translate the research and strategies for brain-compatible math teaching and learning into practical, successful classroom activities. Some general guidelines provide the framework for these activities:

- Writing is an important component in learning mathematics.
- Studies show that more students are motivated and succeed in classes where teachers use activities that address the various intelligences.
- The use of concrete models for representation of concepts and to help create meaning is beneficial.
- Connecting concepts to the real world creates purpose and meaning. This allows math to seem less abstract.
- Using graphic organizers helps students organize their thinking.
- Solving problems in different ways is beneficial to students.

The activities in this book also are supported by research-based rationale for using particular instructional strategies. These strategies include cooperative learning groups, differentiated instruction, discussion, reflection, movement, manipulatives, visualization, and many more, all of which can increase student motivation and retention of learned concepts.

Scientists continue to explore the inner workings of the brain and will likely continue to discover more and more about learning mathematics. Teachers are challenged to stay current on these new findings, to ensure students are using their brains to the fullest capacity. As we learn more about how the brain learns mathematics we can develop activities like those seen in this book, which will

- aid in teachers' presenting meaningful instruction to students in the classroom,
- ensure that students are staying focused and remembering more of what teachers have presented, and
- make teaching and learning more effective and enjoyable experiences.

Teachers should always continue to help students recognize that the learning of mathematics will not only be helpful in their future but allow them to understand and appreciate the wonders of the world each day.

Links to Focal Points and Standards

CONNECTIONS TO FOCAL POINTS

This chart shows the National Council of Teachers of Mathematics focal points covered in each chapter.

Kindergarten

Focal Points		Page Numbers
Number and Operations: Base-Ten System and Place Value	Represent, compare, and order whole numbers and join and separate sets. Use numbers and written numerals to represent quantities. Use numbers and written numerals to solve quantitative problems.	2, 6, 9, 12, 14, 17, 30, 33
Geometry	Understand geometric ideas such as shape, orientation, and spatial relations. Name, identify, and describe two-dimensional and three-dimensional shapes. Use spatial reasoning and shapes to model objects in the environment and to construct more complex shapes.	68, 70, 73, 76, 80, 83, 85
Measurement	Use measurable attributes, such as weight or length, to solve problems by comparing and ordering objects. Compare the lengths of objects directly and indirectly, and order several objects according to length.	100, 103, 106, 108, 111
Data Analysis	Sort objects and use one or more attributes to solve problems. Collect information and data and then count to answer questions about the data.	154, 157, 159, 162, 165
Algebra	Identify, duplicate, and extend simple number patterns and sequential and growing patterns to prepare for creating rules that describe relationships.	138, 141, 143, 146, 149, 151

Grade 1

Focal Points		Page Numbers
Number and Operations and Algebra	Understand addition and subtraction. Use models, including a number line, to solve addition and subtraction problems. Use properties of addition (commutativity and associativity) to add whole numbers. Understand addition and subtraction as inverse operations. Solve two-digit addition and subtraction problems and explain strategies used.	36, 40, 44, 47, 50, 52, 55, 57, 60, 63
Number and Operations	Compare and order whole numbers, and solve problems using these numbers. Group whole numbers as tens and ones. Understand number sequence and represent numbers on a number line.	19, 23, 26
Geometry	Compose and decompose planes and solid figures. Describe shapes by their properties and attributes, and understand how they are alike and different.	88, 90, 95
Measurement and Data Analysis	Solve problems involving measurement and data. Measure by laying units end to end and then counting using tens and ones. Represent measurements and data in bar and picture graphs.	114, 117, 167, 171

CONNECTIONS TO STANDARDS

This chart shows the National Council of Teachers of Mathematics standards covered in each chapter.

Kindergarten

Content Standards		Page Numbers
Number and Operations	Understand numbers, ways of representing numbers, relationships among numbers, and number systems.	2, 6, 9, 12, 14, 17, 30, 33
Algebra	Understand patterns, relations, and functions. Use mathematical models to represent and understand quantitative relationships.	30, 33, 138, 141, 143, 149, 151
Geometry	Analyze characteristics and properties of two- and three-dimensional geometric shapes, and develop mathematical arguments about geometric relationships.	68, 70, 73, 76, 80, 83, 85, 88
Measurement	Understand measurable attributes of objects and the units, systems, and processes of measurement. Apply appropriate techniques, tools, and formulas to determine measurements.	100, 103, 106, 108, 111
Data Analysis and Probability	Formulate questions that can be addressed with data, and collect, organize, and display relevant data to answer them.	154, 157, 159, 162, 165
Representation	Create and use representations to organize, record, and communicate mathematical ideas.	157, 159

Grade 1

Content Standards		Page Numbers
Number and Operations	Understand numbers, ways of representing numbers, relationships among numbers, and number systems. Understand meanings of operations and how they relate to one another.	36, 40, 44, 47, 50, 52, 55, 57, 60
Algebra	Understand patterns, relations, and functions. Use mathematical models to represent and understand quantitative relationships.	19, 23, 26
Geometry	Analyze characteristics and properties of two- and three-dimensional geometric shapes, and develop mathematical arguments about geometric relationships. Apply transformations and use symmetry to analyze mathematical situations. Use visualization, spatial reasoning, and geometric modeling to solve problems.	88, 90, 95
Measurement	Understand measurable attributes of objects and the units, systems, and processes of measurement. Apply appropriate techniques, tools, and formulas to determine measurements.	114, 117, 121, 126, 131
Data Analysis and Probability	Ask questions that can be answered with data, and collect and display data to answer them. Use appropriate methods to analyze data. Develop and evaluate inferences and predictions that are based on data. Understand and apply basic concepts of probability.	167, 171, 175

About the Author

**David A. Sousa, EdD,** is an international consultant in educational neuroscience and the author of seven best-selling books on how to translate brain research into educational practice. For more than 20 years he has presented at national conventions of educational organizations and has conducted workshops on brain research and science education in hundreds of school districts and at colleges and universities across the United States, Canada, Europe, Asia, Australia, and New Zealand.

Dr. Sousa has a bachelor of science degree in chemistry from Massachusetts State College at Bridgewater, a master of arts in teaching degree in science from Harvard University, and a doctorate from Rutgers University. He has taught high school science, has served as a K–12 director of science, and was superintendent of the New Providence, New Jersey, public schools. He has been an adjunct professor of education at Seton Hall University and a visiting lecturer at Rutgers University. He is a past president of the National Staff Development Council.

Dr. Sousa has also edited science books and published articles in leading educational journals. He has received awards from professional associations and school districts for his commitment and contributions to research, staff development, and science education. He is a member of the Cognitive Neuroscience Society, and he has appeared on the NBC *Today* show and on National Public Radio to discuss his work with schools using brain research.

Whole Numbers

SEEING DOTS

Objective

Students will use mental imagery to tell how many dots are on a card.

Anticipatory Set

Show students a photo of one object. Hold it up for 3 seconds, and then place it facedown so students cannot see it. Ask students to name what they saw. Discuss how we can look at something quickly and identify it.

Purpose

Tell students they are going to practice identifying how many dots are on a card. Explain that they should try to find the card as quickly as they can.

Input

Subitizing is best practiced with dot card patterns, rather than with manipulatives, to enhance imagery and eliminate counting by ones.

Before the activity, make a class set of the **Dot Cards reproducibles (pages 4–5).** Cut out each set of cards, and paperclip each set together. Show one card from a set to students, and ask them to say how many dots are on the card. Repeat with other cards from the set. It is important that you only briefly show each card so students do not rely on counting to identify the number of dots. Hold up each card for about 3 seconds.

Modeling

Tell students you are going to give them a set of dot cards. Explain that you will call out a number, and they will quickly find the card that has that number of dots. Model laying out the dot cards faceup. Then say "four," and pick up the dot card with four dots. Hold the card in the air and show students. Say, "I did not count the dots on each card. I quickly glanced at all the cards and picked up the one that had four dots."

Checking for Understanding

Be sure that students understand that they are trying to identify and pick up the correct card as fast as they can.

Guided Practice

Distribute the sets of dot cards. Start out by giving students dot cards 1 through 6. Have students lay their cards faceup. Call out a number between 1 and 6, and ask students to show you that card. Quickly scan the room to see which students are choosing the correct card. Repeat the steps until most students are correctly identifying the cards. Then have students place those cards aside, give them dot cards 7 through 12, and repeat the activity. As students become more proficient, randomly choose any set of six dot cards.

Closure

Tell students to think about what they learned today. Ask them if they had to count the number of dots on each card each time they looked for the matching card or if they just looked at the cards. Invite students to write or dictate one important thing they learned in their math journals.

Independent Practice

Have students place a set of dot cards facedown on their desks. Have them flip over a card and say how many dots are on the card. Have them continue until they have practiced each card a few times.

Dot Cards

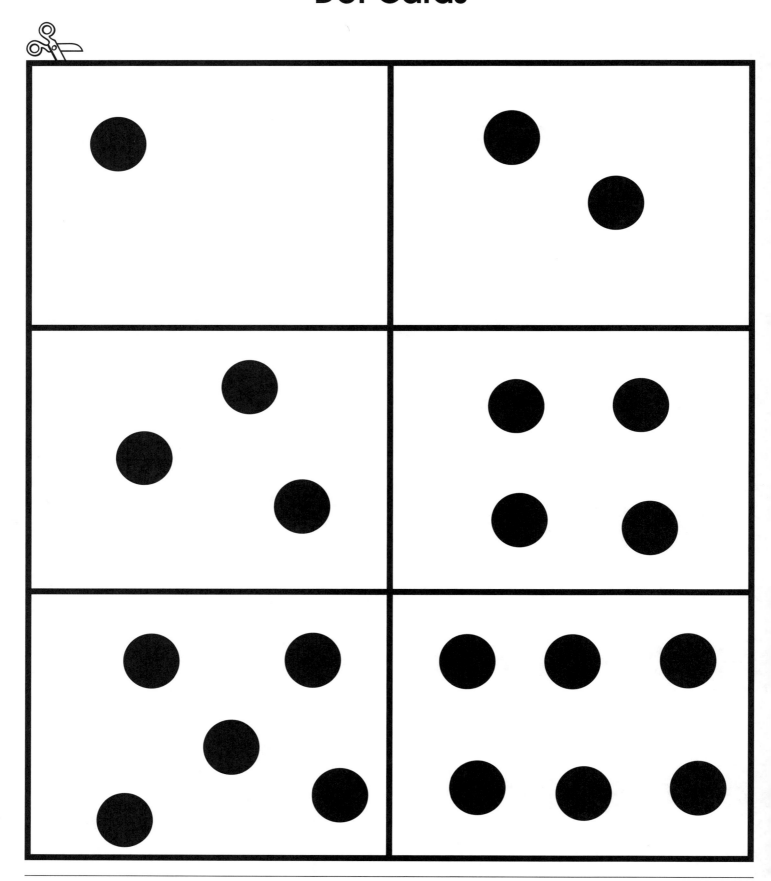

Copyright © 2010 by David A. Sousa. All rights reserved. Reprinted from *Brain-Compatible Activities for Mathematics, Grades K–1*, by David A. Sousa. Thousand Oaks, CA: Corwin, www.corwinpress.com. Reproduction authorized only for the local school site or nonprofit organization that has purchased this book.

Dot Cards

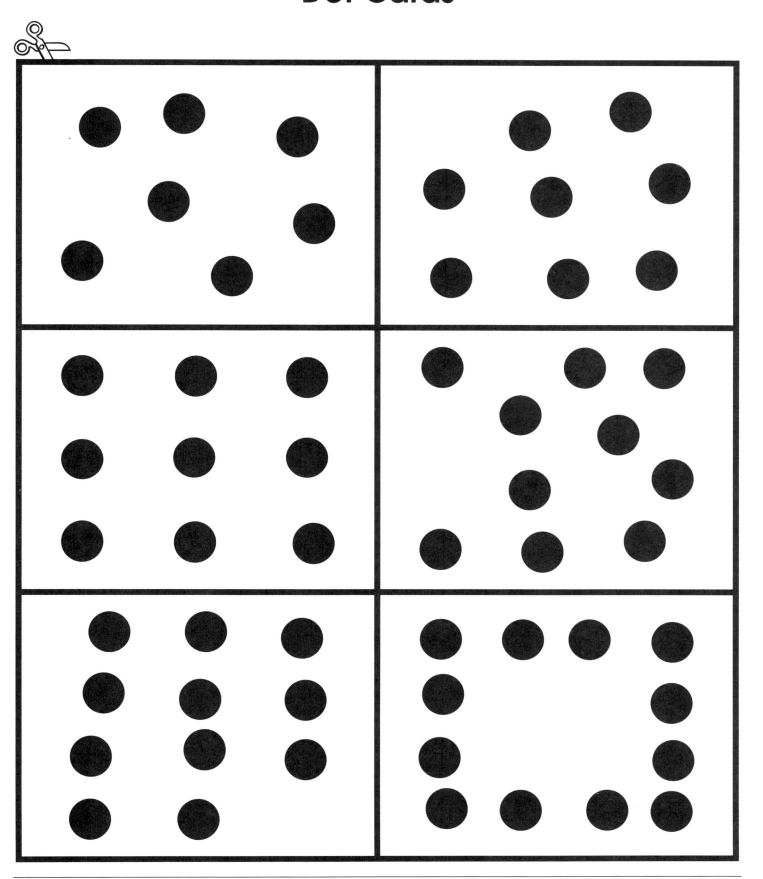

Copyright © 2010 by David A. Sousa. All rights reserved. Reprinted from *Brain-Compatible Activities for Mathematics, Grades K–1*, by David A. Sousa. Thousand Oaks, CA: Corwin, www.corwinpress.com. Reproduction authorized only for the local school site or nonprofit organization that has purchased this book.

HOW MANY?

Objective

Students will count objects using one-to-one correspondence.

Anticipatory Set

Ask one student who is wearing a shirt with buttons to stand up. Point out the buttons and ask aloud, "I wonder how many buttons are on this shirt." Explain that one way to find out is to count the buttons. Point to each button as you count it aloud.

Purpose

Tell students that they will count objects to find out how many there are.

Input

Remind students that when we count objects, we count each object only one time.

Modeling

Use two-sided color chips, or glue two different-colored sheets of construction paper back-to-back, and then cut the paper into small squares. Lay five chips in a row on a table. Have the same color of each chip facing up. Then flip over each chip as you count aloud. Ask students, "How many chips are there? I counted five chips."

Checking for Understanding

Make sure that students understand that the last number counted represents the amount. Flip over three cards. Ask students to point to the square that identifies the quantity.

Guided Practice

Give each student a set of 10 chips. Ask students to place their chips in a row with the same color showing on each chip. Tell students to count the chips. Tell them to turn over each chip as they count it. When they get to the fourth chip say, "Stop." Then ask students, "How many chips did you count?" Repeat the process, stopping at different amounts. Then have students pick up a handful of the chips and count the chips in their hands. Ask them to put their hands behind their backs and ask, "How many chips did you count?"

> Using chips with different-colored sides can enhance students' understanding of the cardinal principle.

Closure

Tell students to follow the directions you give them. Say, "Clap five times." Have students clap and count to five. Repeat with other directions such as, *Stomp your feet four times, Jump up and down six times,* and *Touch your toes three times.* Then ask students to draw a small set of objects in their math journals and count the number of objects. Have them write and complete the sentence frame, "I counted [number of items] [name of item]."

Independent Practice

Give each student a copy of the **Counting Objects reproducible (page 8)** to complete individually. Tell students that they will count the number of objects in each set and then write the number. The objects being counted are of various sizes and in various configurations to represent the concept that number words describe *how many* objects and not their arrangement or size.

Name_____   Date_____

Counting Objects

Directions: Write how many objects are in each set.

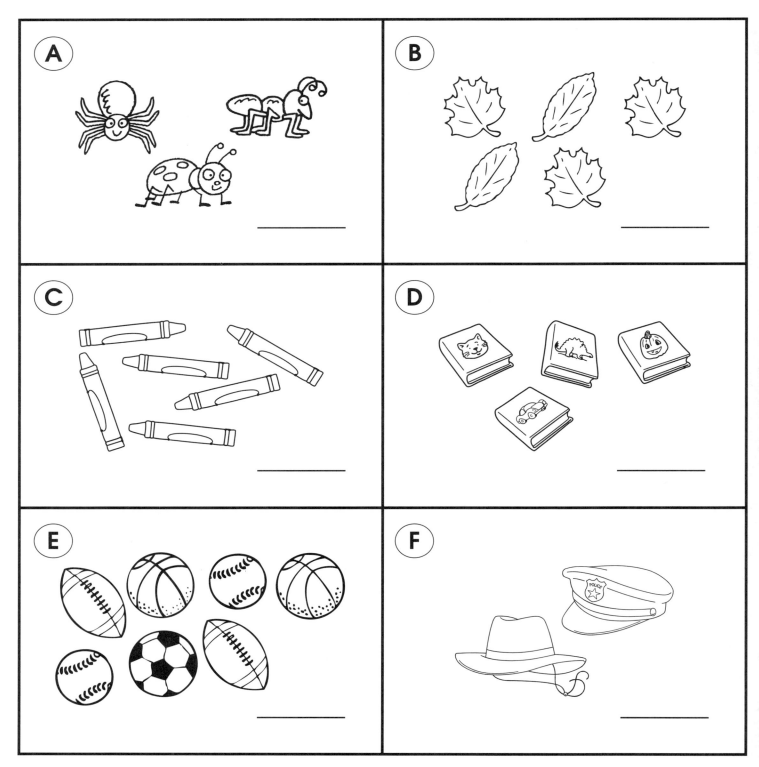

Copyright © 2010 by David A. Sousa. All rights reserved. Reprinted from *Brain-Compatible Activities for Mathematics, Grades K–1*, by David A. Sousa. Thousand Oaks, CA: Corwin, www.corwinpress.com. Reproduction authorized only for the local school site or nonprofit organization that has purchased this book.

NUMBER PATH

Objectives

Students will practice counting forward and backward.

Students will follow navigational directions.

Anticipatory Set

Stand facing the front of the room, and tell students that you will walk forward. Then model walking forward. Now tell them that you will walk backward. Then model walking backward. Next, invite a volunteer to come to the front of the classroom. Invite him or her to suggest another way to move forward and backward, such as skipping, sliding, or hopping. Ask him or her to act out one of these movements along with you.

Purpose

Tell students they will practice counting from 1 to 10 and then backward from 10 to 1.

Input

Review the numerals *1* through *10* and number words *one* through *ten* with students.

Modeling

Write the numerals *1* through *10* on separate index cards or large squares of construction paper. Lay each card in numerical order on the floor to create a path. Step on the first card, and say, "1." Then continue walking on the number path, and count aloud as you step on each card. Stop when you get to the 10th card. Tell students, "I counted from 1 to 10. Now I will walk backward to practice counting backward." Take a step backward, and say, "9, 8, 7," and so on, until you get back to "1."

Checking for Understanding

Make sure students understand that they are to count forward when walking forward and backward when walking backward.

Guided Practice

Divide the class into pairs. Have pairs practice counting and walking on the number path. Afterward, give each pair a **Number Path reproducible (page 11)** and a marker (such as a game piece or a dry bean). Have each pair place its marker on the Start box. Tell students, "Move your marker forward six places." Have partners move their marker six places forward on the game board. Then tell them to move four places backward. Encourage them to count backward aloud. Repeat using different numbers to give students practice moving and counting forward and backward.

Closure

Ask students, "What happened when we moved forward?" (*The numbers got bigger.*) and "What happened when we moved backward?" (*The numbers got smaller.*). Invite them to dictate or write in their math journals about how walking the path helped them to remember to count up or down. Then ask them to write the number words and numerals from 1 through 10.

Independent Practice

Give each student a Number Path reproducible, a die, and a game marker. Tell students to roll their dice and move their markers that many spaces forward. Then have them roll the dice again, and have them move that many spaces backward. Encourage students to continue playing the game until they reach the end of their number paths.

Name_____ Date_____

Number Path

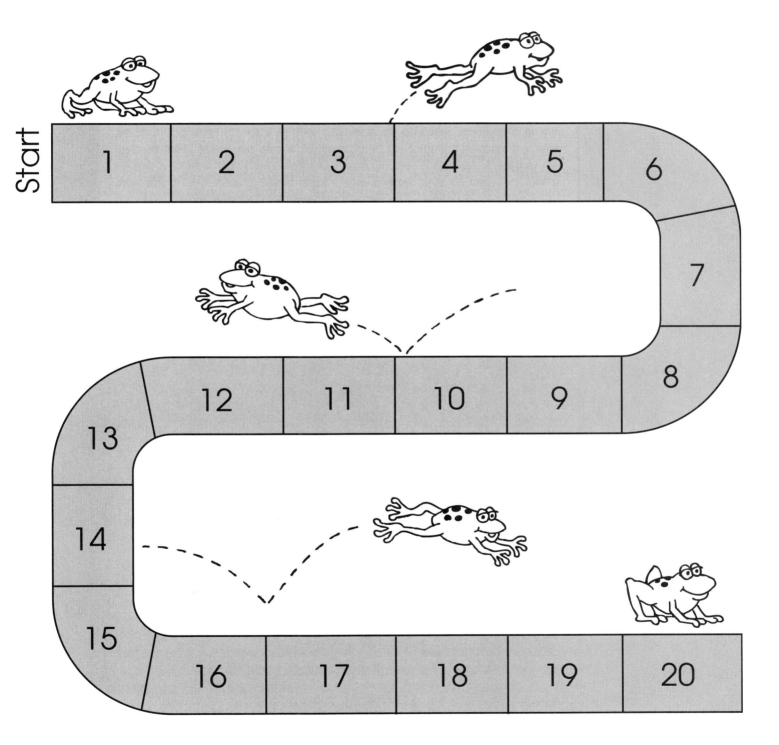

Copyright © 2010 by David A. Sousa. All rights reserved. Reprinted from *Brain-Compatible Activities for Mathematics, Grades K–1*, by David A. Sousa. Thousand Oaks, CA: Corwin, www.corwinpress.com. Reproduction authorized only for the local school site or nonprofit organization that has purchased this book.

COUNTING SETS

Objective

Students will produce sets of objects when given a specific number.

Anticipatory Set

Show students a box of crayons. Explain how crayons come in sets of a given number. Explain that other products, such as packs of gum and boxes of pencils, also come in sets. Explain that the workers who pack these items need to count how many items go in each set.

Purpose

Tell students that they will create sets of objects for a given number.

Input

Remind students that when they count objects for a set, they should count each item only once.

Modeling

Show a paper cup with the number 5 written on it. Arrange several small manipulatives (e.g., counters, buttons, or dried beans) on a table. Count out five manipulatives, and place them in the cup. Then show students a paper cup with the number 7 written on it. Count out seven manipulatives, and place them in that cup.

Checking for Understanding

Make sure students understand how to count objects using one-to-one correspondence. Give each student six crayons, and have them count them for you.

Guided Practice

Divide the class into groups of three or four students. For each group, write a different numeral on each of five separate paper cups. Choose numbers appropriate for your class.

Give each group a set of paper cups and several small manipulatives. Tell groups of students to count the correct number of objects for each cup. When students are finished, have students check to make sure that they have counted correctly by recounting the manipulatives in each cup.

Closure

Ask students to think about why it is important to make sure they count each object only once when counting objects for a set. Have them dictate or write their responses in their math journals.

Independent Practice

Have students fold pieces of paper in fourths. Then have them number the boxes *2* through *5* (top to bottom, right to left). Have students count cereal pieces and glue the correct number of pieces in each box. Encourage more proficient students to use larger numbers.

For more practice, place paper cups numbered *1* through *10* in the math center, along with a bag of dried beans or other small manipulatives. Encourage students to visit the center and work with partners to count the correct number of beans in each cup. Ask partners to check each other's work.

MORE OR LESS

Objective

Students will compare sets of objects and order them using cardinal numbers.

Anticipatory Set

Show students a penny, and tell them, "This is a penny. It is worth 1 cent." Then display 5 pennies and say, "I have 5 pennies. They are worth 5 cents." Explain that pennies are money and can be used to buy things. Say, "If something costs 10 cents, I can pay using 10 pennies."

Purpose

Tell students that they are going to count the number of items in two sets and decide which set has more and which less.

Input

Remind students that *more* means that there will be a larger number of objects and *less* means that there will be a smaller number of objects.

Modeling

Show students a set of five objects and another set of two objects. Count aloud the objects in the first set, and tell students, "There are five objects in this set." Then count the objects in the second set, and say, "There are two objects in this set." Ask students, "Which set has more objects?" Then repeat the numbers *five* and *two*, and say, "Five is more than two, so there are more objects in the first set." Repeat the process with three and four objects. Ask students which set has fewer objects.

Checking for Understanding

Make sure students understand the concept of more or less. Show one finger on your right hand and four fingers on your left hand. Ask students to point to the hand that is showing more fingers. Repeat with three and five fingers, and ask which hand is showing fewer fingers.

Guided Practice

Ask two volunteers to stand next to each other at the front of the classroom. Give one student five pennies and the other student two pennies. Have them hold their coins in one hand and show them to the rest of the class. Ask, "Who has more money?" Then repeat the activity with other volunteers and different numbers of pennies.

Closure

Ask students, "Would you rather have 10 pennies or 7 pennies?" Encourage them to discuss their answers with partners. Then ask students the following question: "A nickel is worth five cents. Write how many pennies you would have if you had two nickels. Draw the number of pennies in your math journal."

Independent Practice

Give students copies of the **More or Less reproducible (page 16).** Tell students that for problems 1 and 2 they should count the number of objects and then draw sets of objects to show more than the given set. For problems 3 and 4, they will draw sets of objects that have less than the given set.

Name_____   Date_____

More or Less

Directions: Draw a set of objects that has **more** than the given set.

A		This set has more.
B		This set has more.

Directions: Draw a set of objects that has **less** than the given set.

C		This set has less.
D		This set has less.

16 Copyright © 2010 by David A. Sousa. All rights reserved. Reprinted from *Brain-Compatible Activities for Mathematics, Grades K–1*, by David A. Sousa. Thousand Oaks, CA: Corwin, www.corwinpress.com. Reproduction authorized only for the local school site or nonprofit organization that has purchased this book.

WHO'S FIRST?

Objective

Students will compare and order sets using ordinal numbers.

Anticipatory Set

Tell students that sometimes we order the steps we use to make something. For example, if we are making a peanut butter and jelly sandwich, first we spread peanut butter on a piece of bread. Second, we spread jelly on top of the peanut butter. Third, we place another piece of bread on top to finish the sandwich.

We also keep track of the order of things. For example, in a race we note who finished first, second, and third. Ask five students to stand in a line. Point to the first person, and explain that he or she is the first one in line. Then repeat by pointing to the second and third students. Ask each of these students to name one thing they do in steps at home or in school. Students might suggest getting ready for bed, setting the table for dinner, and brushing their teeth.

Purpose

Tell students they are going to put items in order using ordinal numbers.

Input

Explain to students that ordinal numbers are similar to cardinal numbers, but we add letters to the end. Write the numerals 1 through 5 on the board. Next to these numbers, write the ordinal numbers 1st, 2nd, 3rd, 4th, and 5th. Point to each number, and say it aloud.

Modeling

Draw the following objects in a row on the board: star, circle, heart, square, and triangle. Tell students as you point to each picture, "The first item is a star. The second item is a circle. The third item is a heart. The fourth item is a square, and the fifth item is a triangle." Then say, "I will erase the fourth item." Erase the square. Say, "Now I will erase the third item." Erase the heart. Finally, say, "I will erase the first item," and erase the star.

Checking for Understanding

Make sure students understand ordinal numbers. Have them clap their hands once, touch their noses, and then stomp their feet. Ask students to repeat the series of actions a few times. Then ask, "What did we do first? What did we do second? What did we do third?" Allow students to respond.

Guided Practice

Give each student five different-colored pieces of O-shaped cereal. Then tell students they are going to place the cereal pieces in a specific order. Direct them to place the green cereal O first. Then tell them to place the yellow cereal O second, the blue cereal O third, the red cereal O fourth, and the purple cereal O fifth. Check that all students correctly ordered their cereal.

Then tell students that they are going to eat the cereal in a specific order. Instruct students to eat the yellow cereal O first, and watch as they eat it. Repeat with the remaining colored cereal pieces. If students are having difficulty with ordering, have them practice just first, second, and third places.

Closure

Tell students to think about the following question: "If you are standing in line waiting to go into a movie theater, would you rather be the first person in line or the fourth person?" Have them explain their answers by writing or dictating a sentence in their math journals.

Independent Practice

Give students drawing paper and crayons. Invite them to draw a line of three characters or animals and explain each one's order in line.

NUMBER SLAP

Objective

Using a number line, students will compare and order whole numbers.

Anticipatory Set

Think of a number between 1 and 10. Without giving any clues, allow one student to try to guess the number. After he or she has guessed the number, ask the class if they think it would have been easier to guess the number if you would have provided them with clues.

Purpose

Tell students that understanding *greater than* and *less than* may seem difficult but that it is just a way of comparing numbers. Then tell them that they are going to practice comparing by numbers by playing a game with a number line and flyswatters.

> Task-related talking is important for learning the vocabulary of mathematics.

Input

Teach students terms such as *greater than, less than, before,* and *after,* and talk about how they would have helped students identify the number more easily during the guessing activity. Teach them the mathematical symbols for *greater than* and *less than.* Draw the symbols on the board, and discuss their meaning. Provide various examples of simple number riddles, such as, Which number is greater than six and less than eight? (*seven*).

Modeling

Draw a large number line on the board. Ask volunteers to help you order the number line from 0 to 20. Make a copy of the **Symbol Swatters reproducible (page 21)** onto cardstock. Tape the greater than symbol to one flyswatter and the less than symbol to another flyswatter.

Tell students that you are going to choose one number between 0 and 20 as your secret number. Their job is to guess the number. To help them guess the number, you will assign two students to be number line "slappers." Slappers will be given the symbol swatters. As numbers are guessed, they will move up and down the number line, helping students to track the secret number.

Model an example. Choose the secret number *9* in your head. Then choose two students to come forward and stand at the start and end of the number line.

Ask a volunteer from the class to guess the number. The volunteer might say the number *3*. Tell the class that *3* is less than your secret number. Guide the student with the less than swatter to slap the number *3* and hold the swatter there. Now students know that the number is between 3 and 20. Perhaps the next student will guess the number *15*. Tell the class that *15* is more than your secret number. Guide the student with the more than swatter to slap *15* and hold the swatter there. Now students know that the number is between *3* and *15*. Repeat until the secret number is guessed.

Ask questions that help students understand that using the greater than and less than hints allows them to guess the secret number more quickly.

Guided Practice

Guide students using multiple examples of Number Slap. Always use "greater than" and "less than" to describe the location of your secret number. Allow each student to have a turn being a slapper, and call on different students to guess your number. Increase difficulty by asking volunteers to add more numbers to the number line until you reach the number *100*.

Independent Practice

Distribute the **Greater Than, Less Than reproducible (page 22),** and have students complete it independently. Encourage them to refer to the number line as needed.

Closure

Invite students to respond to the three journal questions from page *179*. Encourage them to think about how greater than and less than will help them with other math problems.

Symbol Swatters

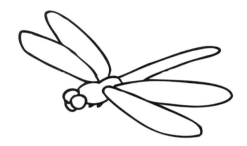

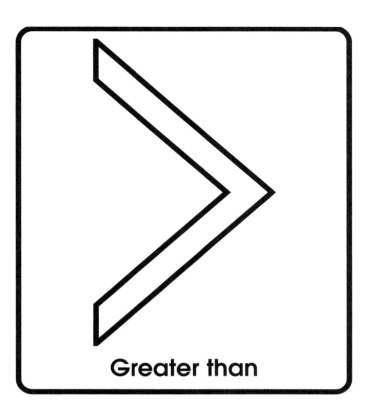

Greater than

Less than

Copyright © 2010 by David A. Sousa. All rights reserved. Reprinted from *Brain-Compatible Activities for Mathematics, Grades K–1*, by David A. Sousa. Thousand Oaks, CA: Corwin, www.corwinpress.com. Reproduction authorized only for the local school site or nonprofit organization that has purchased this book.

Greater Than, Less Than

Directions: Complete the following problems with < or >.

A. 33 ◯ 4   B. 52 ◯ 19

C. 66 ◯ 93   D. 21 ◯ 81

E. 25 ◯ 27   F. 71 ◯ 10

G. 46 ◯ 51   H. 60 ◯ 17

I. 90 ◯ 92   J. 65 ◯ 77

K. 42 ◯ 29   L. 16 ◯ 58

22 Copyright © 2010 by David A. Sousa. All rights reserved. Reprinted from *Brain-Compatible Activities for Mathematics, Grades K–1*, by David A. Sousa. Thousand Oaks, CA: Corwin, www.corwinpress.com. Reproduction authorized only for the local school site or nonprofit organization that has purchased this book.

A TEN COUNT!

Objective

Students will count and group by tens and ones.

Anticipatory Set

Hold up a bunch of 24 flowers, and smell them as you circulate around the room. Let the students smell the flowers while you talk about how multiple flowers are put together in a bunch. Count the flowers aloud. Ask a volunteer to place a rubber band around 10 of the flowers. Ask another volunteer to place a rubber band around 10 more of the flowers. Now count by tens, then ones: "10, 20, 21, 22, 23, 24." Discuss the grouping of tens and ones.

Purpose

Tell students that they are going to practice counting and grouping by tens and ones.

Input

Remind students of the correlation between tens and whole numbers that are divisible by ten. Do this by discussing how many groups of ten can be found in these whole numbers: *10, 20, 30, 40, 50, 60, 70, 80, 90,* and *100.*

Modeling

Model counting and grouping tens and ones using straws or toothpicks. Write the number *36* on the board. Count out 36 straws, then divide them into groups of 3 tens and 6 ones. Use rubber bands or tape to bundle the 3 tens groups together. Make a copy or overhead transparency of the **A Ten Count reproducible (page 25),** and model how to complete the activity. Record the number *36* in the number column. Count the groups of 10 straws, and record that number on the corresponding tens line. Count the single straws, and record that number on the corresponding ones line. Continue to model counting and grouping tens and ones using the numbers *21, 42,* and *59.*

> Activities that are challenging and meaningful develop students' cognitive strengths and raise motivation.

Checking for Understanding

Ask students to come forward and count and group a number using straws. Remind them that for every 10 straws, they must create a bundle (1 "ten"). Record their answers on the reproducible. Answer any questions that remain.

Guided Practice

Distribute a copy of the A Ten Count reproducible to each student along with approximately 50 straws. Alternatively, you could group students in pairs or in small groups of mixed ability levels. Instruct students to decide on a number greater than 10 and write it in the Number column. Then they will count out straws to match the number and group them into tens and ones. They will record the number of tens groups and number of ones on the appropriate lines.

Attaching meaning greatly increases the probability that the learning will be remembered.

Closure

Ask students to write about how grouping by tens and ones might be useful in other parts of their lives.

A Ten Count

Directions: Write the number you chose in the Number column. Sort and record the straws by tens and ones.

Number		
	_____ tens	_____ ones
	_____ tens	_____ ones
	_____ tens	_____ ones
	_____ tens	_____ ones
	_____ tens	_____ ones
	_____ tens	_____ ones
	_____ tens	_____ ones
	_____ tens	_____ ones
	_____ tens	_____ ones
	_____ tens	_____ ones

Copyright © 2010 by David A. Sousa. All rights reserved. Reprinted from *Brain-Compatible Activities for Mathematics, Grades K–1*, by David A. Sousa. Thousand Oaks, CA: Corwin, www.corwinpress.com. Reproduction authorized only for the local school site or nonprofit organization that has purchased this book.

NUMBER JINGLE!

Objective

Students will use musical rhythmic skills to count by twos, fives, and tens.

Anticipatory Set

Getting students' attention for a lesson in mathematics means trying to find an emotional link to the day's learning objective.

Get a set of cheerleading pom-poms, and chant, "Two, four, six, eight! Who do I appreciate? My students! My students! Yeah, students!" Using a similar number pattern with twos, fives, and tens, allow students to create their own chants, for example, "0, 10, 20, 30! I think my socks are dirty! Oh, my! Oh, my! Oh, my!"

Purpose

Tell students that they are going to practice counting by twos, fives, and tens. Tell them that they are going to do this playing a fun singing game.

Input

Explain to students that there are many ways to count other than counting by ones. Counting by twos, fives, or tens can save time. Ask them to tell you about how skip counting is helpful (*telling time, counting money*).

Modeling

Ask the class to sit in a large circle. Begin by teaching students how to clap and then slap their knees in a rhythmic fashion (clap, slap, clap, slap, etc.). Then teach the children the following jingle: "Counting, counting, is so fun! I'm going to count . . . count by ones!"

(clap hands)	(slap knees)
Count-	ing
count-	ing
is	so
fun! (hold)	I'm
going	to
count (hold)	count
by	ones!

Checking for Understanding

Ask students to clap their hands if they know what to do. Provide additional explanation for students who do not clap.

Guided Practice

Guide children through the jingle as they clap their hands and slap their knees. Then explain that this jingle is telling them to count by ones. Explain how the starting student will say "one" on the next clap after the jingle ends. Students will slap their knees, and then the next player to the right will say "two" on the clap, and so on. Use the ones jingle as your warm-up. Then guide students to sing the song and count by twos, fives, and tens (substitute the word *two, five,* or *ten* for the word *one*). As an alternative, say the numbers together as a class.

Closure

In their math journals, have students answer the following question: "What number patterns for counting did you learn today?" Tell students to write some of the patterns in their journals. Use the journal prompts from page 179.

Independent Practice

Have children complete the **Two, Fives, and Tens reproducible (page 28).**

Twos, Fives, and Tens

Directions: Write the missing numbers by counting by twos, fives, and tens.

A. 2, 4, 6, _____, _____, _____, 14 , _____, _____,

_____, 22 , _____, _____, _____, 30 , _____,

_____, _____, _____, 40

B. 5, 10, 15, 20, _____, _____, 35 , _____, _____,

_____, _____, _____, _____, 70 , _____, _____,

_____, 90 , _____, _____

C. 10, 20, _____, _____, _____, 60 , _____, _____,

_____, _____

28 Copyright © 2010 by David A. Sousa. All rights reserved. Reprinted from *Brain-Compatible Activities for Mathematics, Grades K–1*, by David A. Sousa. Thousand Oaks, CA: Corwin, www.corwinpress.com. Reproduction authorized only for the local school site or nonprofit organization that has purchased this book.

2

Addition and Subtraction

COMBINING SETS

Objective

Students will combine sets of objects.

Anticipatory Set

Show students that you have two pencils. Then grab three more pencils from a pencil box. Explain how you had two pencils, then you took three more, so now you have more. Count all the pencils. Explain that when you have one part and add another part, it equals one whole.

Purpose

Tell students that they will combine two sets of objects to create a larger set.

Input

Explain to students that putting two sets of objects together is called combining or adding sets.

Modeling

Use lengths of yarn to make two yarn circles. Then place a large piece of construction paper next to the circles. Place three small items in one circle and two items in the other. You can use plastic animals, blocks, or any other small manipulatives. Explain that you have two sets of items. Tell students, "There are three items in this circle and two items in this circle. I want to combine the items, or put them all together. So I am going to move the items from the first circle and put them on the rectangle."

Place the items on the construction paper. Then say, "I am going to put the items from the second circle on the rectangle too." Place the items from the second circle on the construction paper. Say, "Let's count how many items we have now that I combined the sets." Count the five items aloud. Point to each item as you count it. Explain to students, "I added three items and two items, and now I have five."

Checking for Understanding

Make sure students understand that they are combining, or putting together, two sets. Remind them that we put all the items in the two sets together—we add them together.

Guided Practice

Use yarn or masking tape to create two large circles on the floor. Then use masking tape to make a large rectangle next to the circles. Ask two students to stand in one circle and one student to stand in the other circle. Tell the class to combine the two sets. Ask the students in the circles to move to the rectangle. Have students count aloud the students in the rectangle. Explain, "We had two and added one. Now we have three."

On the board, draw a graphic organizer resembling that on the **Add the Sets reproducible (page 32).** Write "2" in the first circle, "1" in the second circle, and "3" in the rectangle to provide students with a visual representation of what they just did. If students are ready, you can introduce the symbols + and = when you write the numbers in the graphic organizer.

Repeat the process with other sets of students.

Closure

Ask students to describe what happens when we combine sets of objects. Encourage students to draw an example of combining sets in their math journals.

Independent Practice

Give students copies of the Add the Sets reproducible. Explain that for each problem, they will combine the sets of items from the two circles in the rectangle. Remind them that they will draw the number of items from both circles in the rectangle. Then they will need to count how many items there are in the rectangle.

Name_____ Date_____

Add the Sets

Directions: Combine each set of objects. Draw the total number of objects in the rectangle.

A.

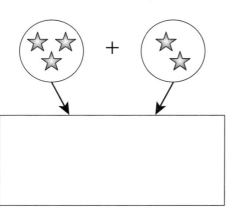

B.

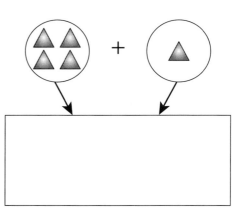

C.

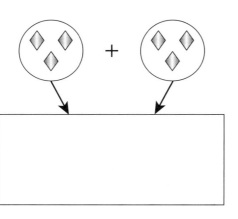

D.

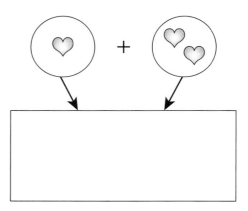

E.

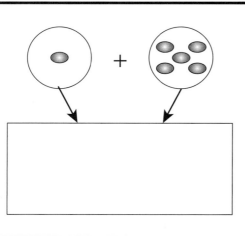

F.

Copyright © 2010 by David A. Sousa. All rights reserved. Reprinted from *Brain-Compatible Activities for Mathematics, Grades K–1,* by David A. Sousa. Thousand Oaks, CA: Corwin, www.corwinpress.com. Reproduction authorized only for the local school site or nonprofit organization that has purchased this book.

SUBTRACTION ACTION

Objective

Students will separate objects in a set.

Anticipatory Set

Ask a group of students to stand together. Walk between the students, and have a few of them move away from the others. Tell the class that you separated the group of students. Then show several stacked Unifix cubes. Break apart the stack, and tell students you separated the set of cubes.

Purpose

Tell students that they will separate, or take away objects from, a set.

Input

Explain to students that when they separate sets, they will be taking some items away from the set.

Modeling

Draw on the board a graphic organizer similar to that on the **Subtraction Action reproducible (page 35).** Draw five objects in the rectangle. Then say, "I want to separate the set. I will take away two objects." Draw two objects in the first circle, and erase two objects in the rectangle. Count how many items are left in the rectangle. Say, "Now there are three objects left." Draw those items in the second circle. Repeat the process by drawing other sets.

Checking for Understanding

Make sure students understand that when they separate objects, they are taking them away. Have students place crayons on their desks. Then tell them to take away two of the crayons.

Guided Practice

Place two hula hoops on the floor, or create two circles using yarn. Use yarn or masking tape to create a large rectangle above the circles so the area looks similar to the Subtraction Action graphic organizer. Ask four students to stand in the rectangle. Then invite the class to separate the set. Ask two students to move to the first circle. Ask the class how many students are left in the rectangle. Then have those two students move to the second circle. Explain: "There were four students, and then two went away. Now there are two left." Write the equation $4 - 2 = 2$ on the board, and repeat the following two sentences: "There were

> Use language to gradually match numbers with objects and symbols.

four students, and then two went away. Now there are two left." As you say the words, point to the numbers and symbols in the equation.

Closure

Ask students what it means to separate objects from a set. Have them draw an example of separating sets in their math journals. Encourage them to dictate or write a sentence explaining their illustrations.

Independent Practice

Give each student a copy of the Subtraction Action reproducible and several small manipulatives. Have them practice separating sets by placing a set of manipulatives in the rectangle and then moving some of the manipulatives to the first circle. Encourage more proficient students to write subtraction equations that correspond to what they did with the manipulatives.

Name_____ Date_____

Subtraction Action

Directions: Show how to separate sets below.

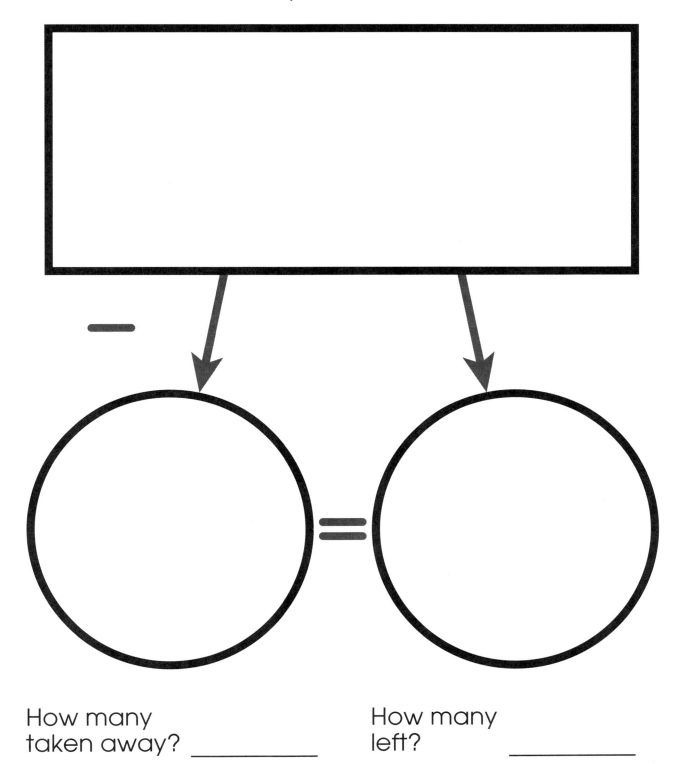

How many
taken away? _____

How many
left? _____

Copyright © 2010 by David A. Sousa. All rights reserved. Reprinted from *Brain-Compatible Activities for Mathematics, Grades K–1*, by David A. Sousa. Thousand Oaks, CA: Corwin, www.corwinpress.com. Reproduction authorized only for the local school site or nonprofit organization that has purchased this book.

SPIN TO WIN

Objective

Students will be able to add whole numbers correctly.

Anticipatory Set

Gain class attention by asking two students from one side of the room to stand, and then ask four students from the other side of the room to stand. Challenge the class to tell how many students are standing in all (*six*). Think aloud and wonder how adding numbers tells us "how many in all": "We had four students and 'counted on' two more—four . . . five, six. I discovered that we have six students in all."

Purpose

Tell students that they will work with a partner to practice an addition strategy using a spinner. Then tell them they will use the "counting-on" strategy.

Input

Ask students to supply answers to the following addition problems: 3 + 2, 6 + 1, and 3 + 4. Pay attention to the strategies students use to solve the equations. Teach or remind students how to use the counting-on strategy for addition.

Show students that putting numbers together is adding. Tell students that one strategy that we can use in adding is counting on from the first number or the larger number. Demonstrate this strategy on the chalkboard.

Modeling

Show students how to play a game using a spinner and addition strategies. Display the **Spinner reproducible (page 38).** Use it to model the game for students. Tell them that the first student will spin his or her spinner, wait until it stops, then call out the number. Then he or she will spin the spinner again, call out the second number, and then say the word *Add!* The partners will compete with each other to be the first to say the correct answer aloud. Model multiple examples for students.

Checking for Understanding

Check for understanding by asking students to hold a thumb up for "I get it" or a thumb down for "I need more explanation."

Guided Practice

Organize the class into pairs, and distribute the Spinner reproducible to each student. Have students play the game, as modeled, spinning and adding the two numbers. Make one copy of the **Team Record Sheet reproducible**

(page 39) for each pair of students, and distribute. Tell students that the winner of each problem should record the number sentence in his or her own column on the reproducible. Circulate around the room, providing assistance and making sure that winners have provided the correct answer to each addition problem.

Independent Practice

Provide an opportunity for students to play the game in a math center or as a whole group. As an alternative, encourage students to bring their spinners home and teach this game to a family member.

Closure

Close the lesson by inviting students to reflect in their math journals. Ask them to write or draw about how they can use the counting-on strategy for other problems.

> Brains respond more than ever to the unique and different—or novelty.

Spinner

Directions: Use a paper clip and a pencil to complete your spinner.

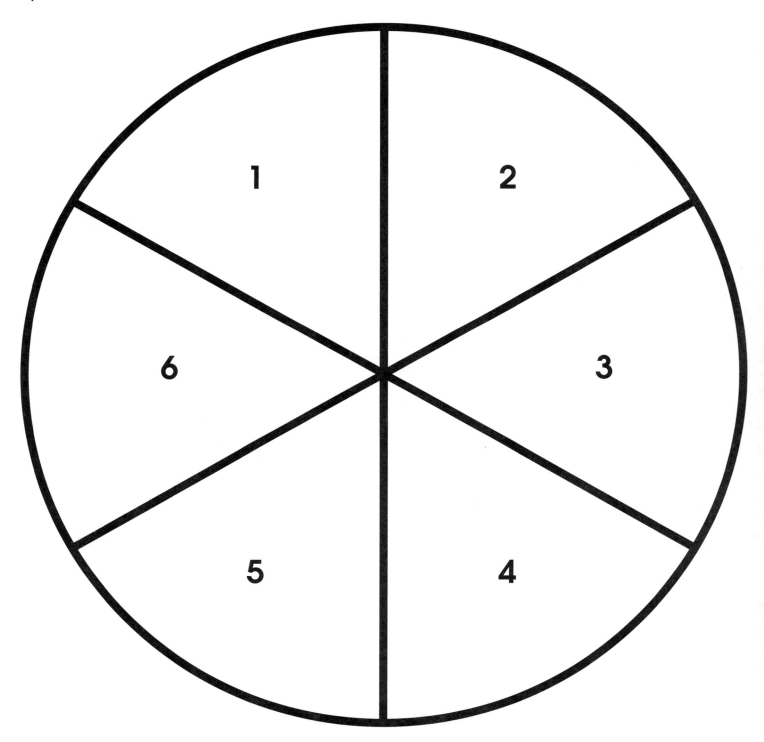

 Copyright © 2010 by David A. Sousa. All rights reserved. Reprinted from *Brain-Compatible Activities for Mathematics, Grades K–1,* by David A. Sousa. Thousand Oaks, CA: Corwin, www.corwinpress.com. Reproduction authorized only for the local school site or nonprofit organization that has purchased this book.

Name_____   Date_____

Team Record Sheet

Directions: Record each problem below.

Player Name #1	Player Name #2
_____	_____
_____ + _____ = _____	_____ + _____ = _____
_____ + _____ = _____	_____ + _____ = _____
_____ + _____ = _____	_____ + _____ = _____
_____ + _____ = _____	_____ + _____ = _____
_____ + _____ = _____	_____ + _____ = _____
_____ + _____ = _____	_____ + _____ = _____
_____ + _____ = _____	_____ + _____ = _____
_____ + _____ = _____	_____ + _____ = _____
_____ + _____ = _____	_____ + _____ = _____
_____ + _____ = _____	_____ + _____ = _____

Copyright © 2010 by David A. Sousa. All rights reserved. Reprinted from *Brain-Compatible Activities for Mathematics, Grades K–1,* by David A. Sousa. Thousand Oaks, CA: Corwin, www.corwinpress.com. Reproduction authorized only for the local school site or nonprofit organization that has purchased this book.

TAKE IT AWAY

Objective

Students will practice subtracting whole numbers.

Anticipatory Set

Without saying why, ask students to put five or six items on their desks. Then tell them you are going to take them away. While doing so, pose questions that help students think about subtraction, for example, *You have a book, two pencils, and a marker on your desk. Altogether you have four items on your desk. If I take away one pencil, how many items do you have left on your desk?* Repeat the process with several students.

Purpose

Tell students that they will be working with partners to practice subtraction strategies by playing a game with dice.

Input

Before playing the game, assess students' level of understanding for subtraction strategies. Remind students that "counting down" is subtraction. Using 10 pencils, create a visual model of the following subtraction problems: $10 - 6, 5 - 2, 7 - 5$, and $8 - 4$. Instruct students as to how to count down from the greater number. Solve the problems. Discuss phrases and terms such as *take away, how many left,* and *minus.*

Modeling

Tell students that they are going to practice using the counting-down subtraction strategy. Start by modeling how to complete the task. Make a copy of the **Number Cards reproducible (page 42)** and the **Take It Away reproducible (page 43)**. Cut apart the number cards. Place the number cards facedown on the desk. Choose one number card, and glue it in the first box on the Take It Away reproducible. Roll a die, and demonstrate how to count the dots. Record the number on the first line of the Take It Away reproducible. Finally, solve the equation, and record the answer on the last line for the first equation.

Checking for Understanding

Check for understanding by asking students to hold a thumb up for "I get it" or a thumb down for "I need more explanation."

Guided Practice

Provide each student with a set of number cards and the Take It Away reproducible. Customize the set of number cards based on students' ability levels. Guide them through two or three problems before encouraging them to work with their partners. This activity also works well as a math center or small-group activity led by an adult. Circulate around the room to make sure students have correctly recorded their numbers and answers. Provide extra guidance for students who may need additional help. Invite questions and sharing about thought processes used during the guided practice.

Independent Practice

Allow students to work in pairs to complete 5 problems each. Once they have completed 10 problems, check their work for accuracy. If appropriate, invite students to practice individually or with an adult helper.

Closure

Invite students to write about the lesson in their math journals. Prompt them to think about counting down as a strategy and how they might use it for other math problems.

Number Cards

6	7	8	9	10
11	12	13	14	15
16	17	18	19	20

6	7	8	9	10
11	12	13	14	15
16	17	18	19	20

42 Copyright © 2010 by David A. Sousa. All rights reserved. Reprinted from *Brain-Compatible Activities for Mathematics, Grades K–1*, by David A. Sousa. Thousand Oaks, CA: Corwin, www.corwinpress.com. Reproduction authorized only for the local school site or nonprofit organization that has purchased this book.

Name_____ Date_____

Take It Away

Directions: Paste a number card to begin the equation. Roll a die and write the number on the first line. Write the answer.

Example: $\boxed{7} - \underline{3} = \underline{4}$

– _____ = _____

– _____ = _____

– _____ = _____

– _____ = _____

– _____ = _____

– _____ = _____

– _____ = _____

– _____ = _____

Copyright © 2010 by David A. Sousa. All rights reserved. Reprinted from *Brain-Compatible Activities for Mathematics, Grades K–1*, by David A. Sousa. Thousand Oaks, CA: Corwin, www.corwinpress.com. Reproduction authorized only for the local school site or nonprofit organization that has purchased this book.

"ALL ABOARD" THE NUMBER LINE

Objective

Students will use a number line to solve addition and subtraction problems.

Anticipatory Set

Gain class attention by pretending to be a train conductor. If you can, get props such as a train whistle and a conductor's hat. Walk around the room shouting, "All Aboard!" Invite students to join the train and follow you in single file around the room. Lead the train outside to the playground. Then create a large number line on the ground using chalk or colored tape. Using a toy train, demonstrate how traveling the number line is a great tool for solving addition and subtraction problems.

Purpose

Tell students that they are going to use a number line to help them solve addition and subtraction problems.

Input

Show students how a number line helps when adding and subtracting numbers. Remind them that adding is counting up and subtracting is counting down. Compare adding and taking away to moving forward and backward on a number line. Demonstrate how adding numbers causes the train to move up the number line, whereas subtracting numbers causes the train to move down the number line.

Modeling

Model how to move the train up and down the number line when adding or subtracting. Place your train on the number 3. Provide students with the problem 3 + 4. Discuss why counting up four places will move the train to 7. Then leave the train on 7. Provide students with the problem 7 − 2. Discuss why counting back two places will cause the train to move to the number 5. Think aloud while demonstrating other addition and subtraction problems.

Checking for Understanding

Ask for volunteers who would like to be the conductors for the train. One by one, ask students to come forward to move the train using simple addition and subtraction problems.

Guided Practice

Distribute a copy of the **Number Line reproducible (page 46)** to each student. Ask students to cut out the small train, and help them thread a pipe cleaner through the holes. Wind the pipe cleaner around the top of a pencil until it is snug. Have students cut out the number line pieces and glue them together to make a number line from 1 to 20. Using various addition and subtraction problems, guide students in using their trains to travel up and down the number line. Encourage them to count aloud each time they move their trains. Use the examples below to guide students to find sums on their number lines.

Model	Example
X + Y = ?	6 + 4 = ?
Start at X	Start at 6
Count up Y	Count up 4
The train ends on X	The train ends on 10
X + Y = Z	6 + 4 = 10

Continue, using the following examples to guide students to find differences on their number line.

Model	Example
Z − Y = ?	10 − 7 = ?
Start at Z	Start at 10
Count down Y	Count down 7
The train ends on X	The train ends on 3
Z − Y = X	10 − 7 = 3

Be creative, and encourage students to have fun. Each time students end on a number, invite them to shout, "All Aboard!" Let them use their imaginations and pretend they are truly conducting this train.

Independent Practice

List three addition problems and three subtraction problems on the board. Tell students to independently solve all six problems, using their number lines as guides. Tell students to record their answers on a separate sheet of paper.

Closure

Invite students to write about the activity and what they learned in their math journals. Encourage them to make a connection to previous activities using counting up and counting down.

Name_____ Date_____

Number Line

Directions: Cut out the number line and train. Using a pipe cleaner, attach your train engine to the top of your pencil. Tape or glue the number line together.

1	2	3	4	5	tape here
6	7	8	9	10	tape here
11	12	13	14	15	tape here
16	17	18	19	20	

46 Copyright © 2010 by David A. Sousa. All rights reserved. Reprinted from *Brain-Compatible Activities for Mathematics, Grades K–1,* by David A. Sousa. Thousand Oaks, CA: Corwin, www.corwinpress.com. Reproduction authorized only for the local school site or nonprofit organization that has purchased this book.

READY, SET . . . ADD!

Objective

Students, using physical activity, will practice adding numbers with a sum between 1 and 12.

Anticipatory Set

Gain class attention by very loudly saying, "Ready, set . . . add!" Display a card with the addition problem 4 + 3. Allow students to share the answer, questioning them about which strategy they used to solve this problem.

Purpose

Tell students that they are going to practice an addition strategy while exercising their bodies. Then tell them that they will be doing this by playing a relay game with their classmates.

Input

Assess students' level of understanding for addition strategies. Ask students to volunteer answers to simple addition problems with sums less than 12. Remind students to use the "counting on from the largest number" strategy for these problems.

Modeling

Tell students that they are going to play a game using addition strategies. Explain that you will divide the class into three team lines. You will give an addition problem to the first student in each line and place the answer cards on the floor in front of them. Students will solve the problems in their heads and then find the answer among the number cards on the floor.

Model by solving the addition problem 4 + 2. Think aloud about the problem: "Four is the larger number, so I will count on two more: four . . . five, six. Now I will find the number 6 card on the floor and hold it in my hand." Demonstrate how to find the answer card on the floor.

Then show students how to pass the chosen answer card by handing the card over their heads or under their legs until it reaches the last student in line. The last student in each line then holds up the card. If the card is correct, the team scores one point. Remind students that after each problem, the first student on each team moves to the last place in line. This allows each student to have a turn to be both first and last.

Checking for Understanding

Invite a volunteer to explain the procedures and clarify any misunderstandings. Be aware of students who appear confused.

Guided Practice

Organize students into three team lines. Play one practice round of the game to be sure that students understand how to the game is played. Then guide students in playing the game. Keep a tally chart on the board, and record points for each team.

Independent Practice

Distribute **Ready, Set . . . Add reproducible (page 49)** for homework that night.

Closure

Invite students to respond to the following in their math journals: "Why is 'counting on from the larger number' a helpful strategy for solving addition problems? In your journal, draw a picture of three apples and six bananas. Circle the larger group. Think about the counting on from the larger number strategy. Find the sum of three apples and six bananas. Write the answer under the picture."

Movement and greater social interaction stimulate long-term memory and create interest in the lesson.

Name_____   Date_____

Ready, Set . . . Add!

Directions: Write the answer to each problem below.

A. 2 + 1 = _____   B. 3 + 4 = _____

C. 4 + 1 = _____   D. 5 + 4 = _____

E. 9 + 2 = _____   F. 8 + 3 = _____

G. 7 + 5 = _____   H. 4 + 4 = _____

I. 8 + 2 = _____   J. 7 + 4 = _____

Copyright © 2010 by David A. Sousa. All rights reserved. Reprinted from *Brain-Compatible Activities for Mathematics, Grades K–1,* by David A. Sousa. Thousand Oaks, CA: Corwin, www.corwinpress.com. Reproduction authorized only for the local school site or nonprofit organization that has purchased this book.

FACT FAMILY TREE HOUSE

Objective

Students will learn about fact families for addition and subtraction.

Anticipatory Set

Remember Tarzan? Give a Tarzan-like yodel, and pretend to swing through the trees. Once you have students' attention, ask them to think about what it would be like to live in the trees. What kind of house would they have in the trees? Would they live with their family in a tree house?

Purpose

Tell students they will learn about fact families for addition and subtraction by using a tree house graphic organizer.

Input

Tell students that there are three numbers in a fact family. Use a human family as an example. Every time the family sits at the table, there is always the same number of people in the family—no matter where the family members sit. With addition fact families, it doesn't matter where the addends are placed; the sum is always the same.

Demonstrate using a simple addition equation. Show students how the sum remains the same when the addends are reversed.

Modeling

Make a transparency of the **Fact Family Tree House reproducible (page 51).** Model how to practice several addition fact families inside the graphic organizer. Think aloud as you complete the organizer.

Guided Practice

Write several groups of numbers on the board. Provide each student with a copy of the Fact Family Tree House reproducible. Prompt students to complete several examples of fact families. Circulate around the room while students are working, and assist as needed. Consider allowing students to work together for additional support.

Closure

Prompt students to write in their math journals about what they learned. Use the prompts from page 179.

Name_____ Date_____

Fact Family Tree House

Directions: Write the fact families in the tree house.

Copyright © 2010 by David A. Sousa. All rights reserved. Reprinted from *Brain-Compatible Activities for Mathematics, Grades K–1*, by David A. Sousa. Thousand Oaks, CA: Corwin, www.corwinpress.com. Reproduction authorized only for the local school site or nonprofit organization that has purchased this book.

MATH DETECTIVE

Objective

Students will understand the inverse relationship of addition and subtraction.

Anticipatory Set

> The learning episode begins when the learner focuses on the teacher with intent to learn.

Gain class attention by holding up a magnifying glass. Walk around the room pretending to investigate various objects and students, including students' fingerprints. Then write the following problems on the board: $3 + 7 = 10$, $10 - 3 = 7$, and $10 - 7 = 3$. Tell students to imagine that they are a group of detectives. Ask them to investigate the problems that are written on the board. Think aloud about how understanding inverse relationships can help us in real-life math situations.

Purpose

Tell students that they are going to be math detectives to discover the inverse relationship of addition and subtraction.

Input

Show several addition problems on the board. Encourage students to come forward and talk about and solve each problem. Then write the inverse relationships next to the addition problems. Point out the patterns in these problems.

Modeling

Make a copy of the **Funny Fingerprints reproducible (page 54),** and cut out the fingerprints. Model how to create an addition equation using the fingerprints as manipulatives. Think aloud as you model the following: "Three fingerprints plus four fingerprints equals how many fingerprints? I'll put three fingerprints here and count (add) four more. Now I have seven altogether. Let's see what the inverse relationship is. I have seven fingerprints altogether. If I take away (subtract) four, I have three fingerprints left."

Continue modeling by writing your sample equation on the board. Repeat your think-aloud, and refer to the fingerprints. Show the inverse relationship on the board, and encourage students to ask questions and share their own discoveries.

Guided Practice

Make a copy of the Funny Fingerprints reproducible for each student, and ask the students to cut out the shapes. Guide the class through two or three example equations, using the fingerprints as manipulatives. Once the students have the hang of it, guide them through two more, this time recording the equations on paper. Invite questions, and monitor students carefully during guided practice.

Checking for Understanding

Make sure students understand the inverse relationship of addition and subtraction. Check for understanding by asking volunteers to demonstrate sample problems using the fingerprint manipulatives and the board.

Independent Practice

Instruct students to complete five inverse-relationship equations and record their work on sheets of paper. Consider creating groups of students with mixed abilities.

Closure

Ask students to respond to the journal prompts from page 179.

Name_____ Date_____

Funny Fingerprints

Directions: Cut out the fingerprints, and use them to help you add or subtract.

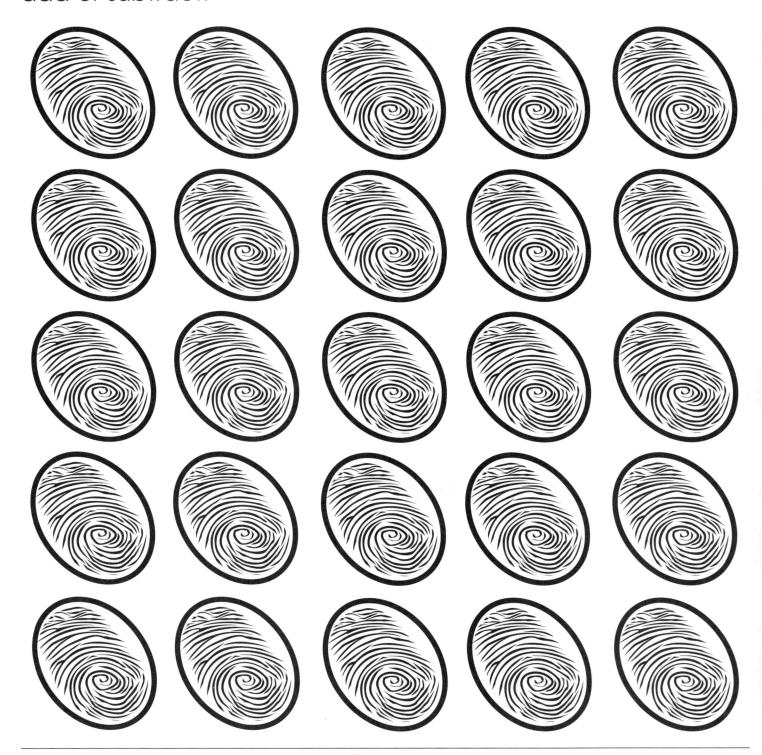

54 Copyright © 2010 by David A. Sousa. All rights reserved. Reprinted from *Brain-Compatible Activities for Mathematics, Grades K–1*, by David A. Sousa. Thousand Oaks, CA: Corwin, www.corwinpress.com. Reproduction authorized only for the local school site or nonprofit organization that has purchased this book.

FLIP IT!

Objective

Students will understand the inverse relationship of addition and subtraction.

Anticipatory Set

Ask students to think about their favorite games. Encourage them to talk about what they like about the games and any lessons they learn while playing them.

Purpose

Tell students they are going to learn about inverse relationships in addition and subtraction.

Input

Teach students about the factors in addition and subtraction equations. Use correct terminology when identifying the factors. Explain how the equal sign means equality or balance. The same thing is done on both sides of the equal sign. Demonstrate this by writing an addition equation on the board ($3 + 2 = 5$). Then show students how the inverse is also true ($2 + 3 = 5$). Finally, show how you can rearrange the numbers to make a subtraction problem ($5 - 3 = 2$).

Modeling

Gather the following materials:

About 12 small wooden dowels ($6'' \times 1''$)

About 12 rulers

Index cards

Write various addition and subtraction equations on index cards. Make enough so each student in the class has at least three.

Demonstrate how to play Flip It! Place a dowel on the table, and balance a ruler on top like a seesaw. Lay one index card on one end of the ruler. Tap the other end of the ruler to make the card flip in the air. When the card lands, read the equation aloud. Then recite the inverse relationship of the equation.

Checking for Understanding

Use a thumbs-up or thumbs-down technique to check for understanding.

> New learning should be practiced frequently at first so that it is quickly organized (massed practice).

Guided Practice

Organize the class into pairs, and give students the opportunity to play Flip It! Remind them how to play the game, and suggest that several students practice while the rest of the class watches.

While the students play the game, circulate around the room, and assist as needed. Help students with the inverse relationships, and make sure to assess the ability levels of all students.

Closure

Prompt students to think about what they learned about inverse relationships. Invite them to write in their math journals about how inverse relationships will help them with addition and subtraction.

NUMBER GRID

Objective

Students will add and subtract two-digit numbers using a number grid.

Anticipatory Set

Gain class attention by quickly solving two-digit addition and subtraction problems, for example, $45 - 22 = 23$, $74 + 15 = 89$, and $96 - 23 = 73$. Continue to recite quickly these types of problems. Talk to students about whether they think they can solve these types of two-digit addition and subtraction problems. Ask students to brainstorm different tools, or strategies, that could help them in solving these types of problems. Students may suggest number lines, calculators, manipulatives, and number grids.

Purpose

Tell students that they are going to solve two-digit addition and subtraction problems by using a number grid and playing a fun game with their classmates.

Input

Before beginning the game, display a transparency of the **Number Grid reproducible (page 59)** using your overhead projector. Draw a connection between using a number line and using a number grid. Review the concepts involving adding and subtracting on a number grid. Have students create their own number grids, or use prepared hundred charts.

> Charts in different arrangements offer many opportunities for students to explore number patterns.

Modeling

Ask students to look at the number grid. Write the number sentence $43 - 27 = ?$ on the board. Tell students to start at 43, placing their fingers on the 43 as you do the same. Subtract 20 by moving your finger up two rows to 23. Have students repeat after you. Now subtract 7 more by counting back from 23; have students do the same. End on the 16 square. Point out that during the game, you will be saying the number problems, and students will be solving the problems using this method.

Checking for Understanding

Ask students to solve various addition and subtraction problems using their number grids. Use the thumbs-up technique to check for understanding.

Guided Practice

Divide the class into groups of three. Provide each group one quarter and two piles of number cards showing numbers *1* through *5*. Distribute one

Vary the contexts in which the practice is carried out to maintain interest.

Number Grid reproducible and a marker (e.g., penny, game piece) to each student. Explain to groups that students will be competing against one another to get to 100 on their number grids. Tell students to begin by placing their markers on 0. Tell them that each player in their group will take turns choosing two cards from the number piles. The first player will draw two cards, then put the cards together to create a two-digit number. The player will move the marker to that number. Then the player will flip the quarter. Heads means the player will add the next number drawn. Tails means the player will subtract the next number drawn. The player then draws the next two-digit number and adds it to or subtracts it from the first number, placing the marker on the sum or difference. If all players agree that the answer is correct, the next player will take a turn. After all three players have taken their turns, the player who is on the highest number wins. The first person to win three rounds wins the game.

Independent Practice

Have each student take his or her number grid home and practice this game with a family member.

Closure

Provide students with their math journals, and ask them to write about what they learned during the lesson.

Name_____   Date_____

Number Grid

1	2	3	4	5	6	7	8	9	10
11	12	13	14	15	16	17	18	19	20
21	22	23	24	25	26	27	28	29	30
31	32	33	34	35	36	37	38	39	40
41	42	43	44	45	46	47	48	49	50
51	52	53	54	55	56	57	58	59	60
61	62	63	64	65	66	67	68	69	70
71	72	73	74	75	76	77	78	79	80
81	82	83	84	85	86	87	88	89	90
91	92	93	94	95	96	97	98	99	100

Copyright © 2010 by David A. Sousa. All rights reserved. Reprinted from *Brain-Compatible Activities for Mathematics, Grades K–1*, by David A. Sousa. Thousand Oaks, CA: Corwin, www.corwinpress.com. Reproduction authorized only for the local school site or nonprofit organization that has purchased this book.

LET'S GO, DOMINO!

Objective

Students will use commutativity and associativity to add whole numbers in connection to fact families.

Anticipatory Set

Emotion drives attention, and attention drives learning.

Play a shortened version of the song "We Are Family" by The Pointer Sisters as a way to get students' attention. Get students to dance and sing along if they are familiar with the lyrics.

Purpose

Tell students that they are going to play a game using dominos to help them understand and identify fact families.

Input

Before beginning the lesson, remind students of the basic laws of addition and subtraction. Remind them that if $a + b = c$, then $b + a = c$. Think aloud about how $8 + 4 = 12$ and $4 + 8 = 12$. Use manipulatives to demonstrate the relationship of these two problems. Repeat with related subtraction sentences. Tell students that these are called *fact families* and all the numbers can be used to create two addition equations and two subtraction equations.

Modeling

Tell students that they are going to play a game using dominos to help them identify fact families. Demonstrate the game by displaying a domino. Show students how the domino is divided into two sides. Tell them that you will count the dots on the first side of your domino (4). Then count the dots on the second side (3). Record these numbers on the board. Tell students that fact families contain three numbers. To find the third number, you must add these two numbers (7). Record the sum on the board. Then tell students that from these three numbers, you will be able to write a fact family consisting of two addition problems and two subtraction problems. Write the fact family on the board:

Fact Family

$4 + 3 = 7$	$7 - 3 = 4$
$3 + 4 = 7$	$7 - 4 = 3$

Guided Practice

Divide the class into teams of four, and assign each member of the team a number, one through four. Explain that each team will be given one chalkboard, one piece of chalk, and one bag of dominos. Tell students that you will say, at the start of each round, "Let's go, domino!" and call out one of the team members' numbers (e.g., "number two"), designating that member as the round's team leader. At this time, that player will pull one domino from the team's bag. The player will display the domino, and the group will quickly count the dots on the domino and add the two numbers. Once the group has discovered the sum, the team leader will write only the three numbers at the top of the chalkboard (e.g., "2, 4, 6").

This early practice (referred to as *guided practice*) is done in the presence of the teacher, who can now offer immediate and corrective feedback to help students analyze and improve their practice.

Next, the leader will quickly pass the board and chalk to the next player. That player will write the first addition fact for this family on the board. He or she will pass the board and chalk to the next player, who will write the other cumulative addition sentence. The game will continue with the next player's writing the first related subtraction fact, and the round will end when the team leader writes the final related subtraction fact. At this time, the team leader will stand and present the chalkboard to you, the teacher. If students have provided correct number sentences for that fact family, they will be awarded one point. Tally points on the board. After all boards have been checked, a new round begins with a new team leader.

Checking for Understanding

Make sure each team understands that if it has an incorrect answer when you check its chalkboard, the team must correct its mistakes (the team leader is in charge of the board, the chalk, and erasing during correcting time). The team leader stands when the team is ready for a recheck.

Independent Practice

To encourage intrapersonal skills, ask students to return to their desks and enjoy playing the same game alone. Distribute a copy of the **Let's Go, Domino! reproducible (page 62)** and three dominos to each student. This time, students will solve the sum of the dominos and list the four fact family sentences on their reproducibles independently.

Closure

Instruct students to illustrate a domino and write the four number sentences for the corresponding fact family in their journals. Encourage them to respond to the journal prompts from page 179.

Name_____   Date_____

Let's Go, Domino!

Directions: Draw the dots on the dominos below. Then write the fact families.

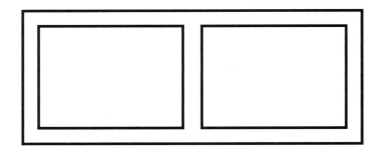

_____ + _____ = _____

_____ + _____ = _____

_____ − _____ = _____

_____ − _____ = _____

_____ + _____ = _____

_____ + _____ = _____

_____ − _____ = _____

_____ − _____ = _____

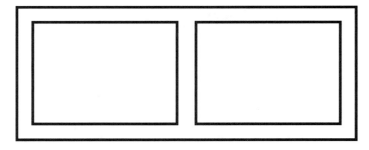

_____ + _____ = _____

_____ + _____ = _____

_____ − _____ = _____

_____ − _____ = _____

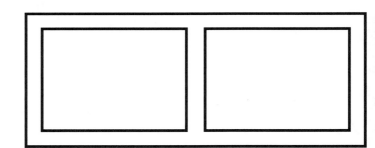

_____ + _____ = _____

_____ + _____ = _____

_____ − _____ = _____

_____ − _____ = _____

62 Copyright © 2010 by David A. Sousa. All rights reserved. Reprinted from *Brain-Compatible Activities for Mathematics, Grades K–1,* by David A. Sousa. Thousand Oaks, CA: Corwin, www.corwinpress.com. Reproduction authorized only for the local school site or nonprofit organization that has purchased this book.

GUIDE TO PROBLEM SOLVING

Objective

Students will use a graphic organizer to work through problem solving.

Anticipatory Set

Set out familiar math manipulatives so students can see them. Think aloud as you decide how to add 27 + 32. Use the manipulatives if necessary, but most important, talk through the strategy you use to complete the equation.

Purpose

Tell students they will learn how to use a graphic organizer to help them solve a math problem.

Input

Explain to students that there are many tools we can use to solve problems. For example, we can use tools such as manipulatives, blank paper and a pencil, graphic organizers, and calculators. Sometimes we use several tools to solve a problem. Explain that today we will be using a graphic organizer.

Modeling

Make an overhead transparency of the **Guide to Problem Solving reproducible (page 65).** Demonstrate how to complete the organizer using a simple addition problem. Think aloud as you talk through each step of the task. Make sure you clearly explain each step of the process and articulate why you are doing what you are doing. Talk about how using a graphic organizer can help students organize their thinking and make it easier for them to understand math problems.

Guided Practice

Give each student several copies of the Guide to Problem Solving reproducible. Complete one full organizer together as a class while you demonstrate on the board or overhead. Use a simple addition problem to guide students through the process without confusing them about the computation.

Closure

Invite students to share their graphic organizers with partners. Then invite volunteers to share with the entire class. Discuss how various strategies are acceptable, and encourage students to talk about what they did and why they did it. Prompt students to explain their learning in their math journals and make a connection to other things they have learned in math.

Collect the organizers from the students, and review them carefully. They will provide important clues about students' development of mathematical thinking and give you an opportunity to anticipate students' needs. Use what you discover about your students to support their learning as they grow in mathematical processing. Adjust lessons to address various strategies and work with students' individual strengths.

Independent Practice

Next, encourage students to work with partners or individually (as appropriate) to complete another organizer using a more complex equation. Remind students that they may use any strategy they wish to figure out the answer, but they must fill in all parts of the graphic organizer.

Name_____ Date_____

Guide to Problem Solving

Directions: Complete the graphic organizer using a math problem.

Understand	Plan
What do you know? What do you have to do? 	How will you do it?
Solve	**Check**
What is the answer? 	How can you check your work? Is it correct? 

Copyright © 2010 by David A. Sousa. All rights reserved. Reprinted from *Brain-Compatible Activities for Mathematics, Grades K–1*, by David A. Sousa. Thousand Oaks, CA: Corwin, www.corwinpress.com. Reproduction authorized only for the local school site or nonprofit organization that has purchased this book.

3

Geometry

Shifting Shapes

Feel the Shapes

Shape Sort Race

Fishing for Triangles

3-D Shapes

Shape Up

Shapes Everywhere

The Art of Shapes!

Smart Shapes

The Shape Museum

SHIFTING SHAPES

Objective

Students will listen to descriptions of shapes and identify them.

Anticipatory Set

Hold up a pencil, and describe it to the class. Tell students, "This object is long and thin. It has an eraser on one end and a point on the other. It is yellow." Explain that you described what a pencil looks like. Next, describe another common classroom object. Invite students to guess the object you're describing. As time allows, invite volunteers to describe objects while their classmates guess.

Purpose

Tell students they will describe and name shapes.

Input

Draw several simple shapes on the board, such as a square, a rectangle, a triangle, a circle, and an oval. Say the name of each shape, and review its characteristics. For example, identify the number of sides. Point out any corners or angles.

Modeling

Explain to students that you will describe a shape as you form it with a pipe cleaner. Begin with a square and say, "This shape has four equal sides. It has four corners." Fold the pipe cleaner into fourths. Join the two ends of the pipe cleaner together to create a square. Hold up the shape you created and say, "It is a square."

Checking for Understanding

Show a square, and ask students to point to a side. Then ask them to point to a corner.

Guided Practice

Have students make shapes with pipe cleaners as you describe the characteristics of each shape. For example, for a triangle, say, "This shape has three sides and three corners." Encourage students to fold their pipe cleaners into thirds to create a triangle. Ask them to hold up their shapes and identify them by name. If students have difficulty folding pipe cleaners, you may ask them to draw the shapes instead. As time permits, repeat the process using several shapes.

Closure

Ask students to draw one or two shapes in their math journals. Then have them write or dictate a description of the shape, such as size, number of sides, number of corners, and so on.

Independent Practice

Give students several pipe cleaners. Invite them to bend the pipe cleaners into various shapes. Then ask them to share their shapes with partners. Have partners describe their shapes to each other. Then distribute construction paper and glue. Invite partners to glue their shapes to the construction paper to make an artistic shape picture. Ask each pair to share its artwork with the class and identify the shapes used.

FEEL THE SHAPES

Objective

Students will identify two-dimensional shapes.

Anticipatory Set

Describe the physical traits of a student in the class without saying his or her name. Ask students to identify who you are describing. Afterward, explain to students that they identified the person by listening to a description of his or her appearance.

Purpose

Tell students that they are going to identify shapes by feeling them.

Input

Remind students of the names of simple shapes. Show paper cutouts of one shape at a time. Identify the number of sides on the shape, and point out any other special features, such as one side's being longer than the others or all sides being equal.

Modeling

Place pattern blocks or several cutout shapes, such as circles, triangles, squares, and rectangles, in a drawstring bag or covered box. Put one hand in the bag without looking inside. Explain to students that you are grabbing and feeling one shape. Describe how you are feeling the sides of the shape. For example, say, "I am feeling the edges of the shape. It has four sides. Two sides are longer than the other two sides. This shape must be a rectangle." Pull out the shape, and show it to the students. Ask the class if you were correct.

Checking for Understanding

Make sure students know the name of each shape and the number of sides it has.

Guided Practice

Organize students into groups of three or four. Give each group a bag of shapes. Have students take turns reaching into the bag and grabbing one shape. Remind them to feel the shape and identify it before removing it from the bag. Then have the student take out the shape to verify that he or she named it correctly.

Closure

To review the characteristics and name of each shape, give each student a copy of the **Shape Bingo reproducible (page 72)** and several game markers (e.g., dried beans, counters, or small paper squares). Explain that the class is going to play a Bingo game to review the shapes. Briefly review how to play Bingo in case some students do not know how to play.

Ask students to draw one shape in each box on their Shape Bingo reproducibles. Tell them to draw a triangle, a square, a rectangle, a circle, a hexagon, a heart, an oval, and a trapezoid. Then begin the game by describing a shape. Have students place a game marker on that shape on their Shape Bingo reproducibles. Repeat the process using different shapes until you have described each shape. The first student to mark three shapes in a row vertically or horizontally calls out "Bingo!" If the student has marked all of the shapes correctly, he or she wins the game. Play several rounds of the game as time allows.

Independent Practice

Have students draw in their math journals a picture of an object that uses two or more shapes. Some suggestions are a house, a train, and an ice cream cone. Have students label their pictures and list the shapes they used to create them.

Name_____ Date_____

Shape Bingo

   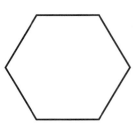

	Free Space	

  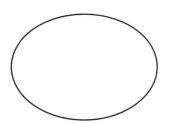 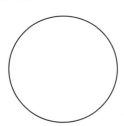

72 Copyright © 2010 by David A. Sousa. All rights reserved. Reprinted from *Brain-Compatible Activities for Mathematics, Grades K–1*, by David A. Sousa. Thousand Oaks, CA: Corwin, www.corwinpress.com. Reproduction authorized only for the local school site or nonprofit organization that has purchased this book.

SHAPE SORT RACE

Objective

Students will count the sides of shapes and sort the shapes by the number of sides.

Anticipatory Set

Show students a book. Explain that the book has four sides. Point to each side as you count aloud. Then point out other common classroom objects, and ask students to identify the number of sides on each one.

Purpose

Tell students they are going to count the number of sides on certain shapes and sort those shapes into groups.

Input

Before the activity, write the numerals *0, 3,* and *4* on separate index cards. Place each card on an empty box or basket. Place several cutout shapes of rectangles, squares, circles, trapezoids, and triangles in a box. Make another collection with the same number of shapes, and place it in another box. Show students the number boxes; point to each number and identify it. Tell them, "This basket has the number *0* on it." Show students one of the shape boxes, and pull several shapes from it. Remind students that shapes have different numbers of sides and that some shapes have no sides.

Modeling

Choose one shape from a shape box. Model how to count the number of sides on the shape. Point to each side as you count aloud. Say, "One, two, three. This triangle has three sides." Then walk to the number box with a *3* on it. Say, "This box has a *3* on it. Because this triangle has three sides, I am going to place it in this box."

Explain that you will divide the class into two teams. Each team member will choose one shape from the shape box, count the sides, and place the shape in the appropriate number box. Continue to model the activity using one or two more shapes.

Checking for Understanding

Make sure that team members understand they are trying to match the number of sides on their shapes to the numbers on the boxes. Have students point to the number *0* box, the number *3* box, and the number *4* box several times while saying the numbers aloud.

Guided Practice

Studies show that more students are motivated and succeed in classes where teachers use activities that address the various intelligences.

Divide the class into two teams. Have each team form a line. Place one shape box next to each team. Place the number boxes several feet away from the teams. When you say "Go," have the first member of each team choose one shape from the box. Then have him or her place the shape in the appropriate number box. Have each team member repeat the procedure. The first team to finish wins.

At the end of the race, gather the number boxes. Hold the number *0* box and say, "All the shapes in this basket should have zero sides." Pull out some of the shapes, and verify that they have zero sides. Do the same for the number *3* and *4* boxes.

Closure

Have students return to their seats. Show them another shape, and ask them to quietly name the shape. Then have them tell how many sides that shape has by holding up the same number of fingers. Then ask students to identify two classroom objects and their shapes. Have them draw a picture of each object in their math journals, such as a clock (circle) and a book (rectangle). Have them label each picture with the number of sides.

Independent Practice

Give students a copy of the **Counting Sides reproducible (page 75)** to complete individually. Explain that students will be drawing pictures of shapes based on the number of sides: zero, three, and four.

Counting Sides

Directions: Draw pictures of shapes that have **0, 3,** and **4** sides.

0 Sides	3 Sides

4 Sides

Copyright © 2010 by David A. Sousa. All rights reserved. Reprinted from *Brain-Compatible Activities for Mathematics, Grades K–1,* by David A. Sousa. Thousand Oaks, CA: Corwin, www.corwinpress.com. Reproduction authorized only for the local school site or nonprofit organization that has purchased this book.

FISHING FOR TRIANGLES

Objective

Students will identify shapes in different sizes.

Anticipatory Set

Show students a pen. Then show them another pen that looks different from the first one. Ask students if the pens look the same. Explain that even though the pens are not exactly alike, they are both called pens.

Purpose

Tell students they are going to look for triangles.

Input

Remind students that triangles have three sides. Draw examples of various triangles on the board. Point out that some look a little different from others but they are all triangles.

Modeling

Place a large plastic hoop (hula hoop) on the floor to create a "pond." Cut out several paper shapes, including various triangles, and clip a paperclip to each shape. Lay the shapes within the hoop. Create "fishing poles" by attaching one end of a length of yarn to a wooden dowel. Tie the other end of the yarn to a small magnet.

Use one of your fishing poles to model how to "fish" for triangles. Tell students you are searching for triangles in the pond. Place your fishing pole over a triangle. The magnet should attract the paperclip on the triangle. Then carefully lift the triangle from the pond.

Checking for Understanding

Make sure students understand that triangles have three sides and can look different from one another.

Guided Practice

Invite students to take turns fishing for triangles. You can make a few fishing poles so several students can fish at the same time. Or you can create a few ponds and fishing poles and place a small group at each pond. Have students create a pile of the triangles they catch. If they catch shapes that are not triangles, direct them to place those shapes back in the pond (or "throw them back"). At the end of the activity, allow students to take turns showing the class the triangles that they caught.

Closure

Ask students to think about what a triangle looks like. Have them draw several triangles in their math journals. Ask students to dictate or write a sentence about their triangles, such as, *All triangles have three sides.*

Independent Practice

Give students crayons and copies of the **Find the Triangles and Squares** and **Find the Rectangles and Circles reproducibles (pages 77–78)** to complete individually. Explain that they will be identifying and tracing triangles, squares, rectangles, and circles. Allow students plenty of time to complete the reproducibles. To add more challenge, have students trace each shape in a different color, such as triangles—red, squares—green, rectangles—blue, and circles—orange.

Name_____ Date_____

Find the Triangles and Squares

Directions: Trace the triangles and squares in the picture.

Copyright © 2010 by David A. Sousa. All rights reserved. Reprinted from *Brain-Compatible Activities for Mathematics, Grades K–1*, by David A. Sousa. Thousand Oaks, CA: Corwin, www.corwinpress.com. Reproduction authorized only for the local school site or nonprofit organization that has purchased this book.

Name_____ Date_____

Find the Rectangles and Circles

Directions: Trace the rectangles and circles in the picture.

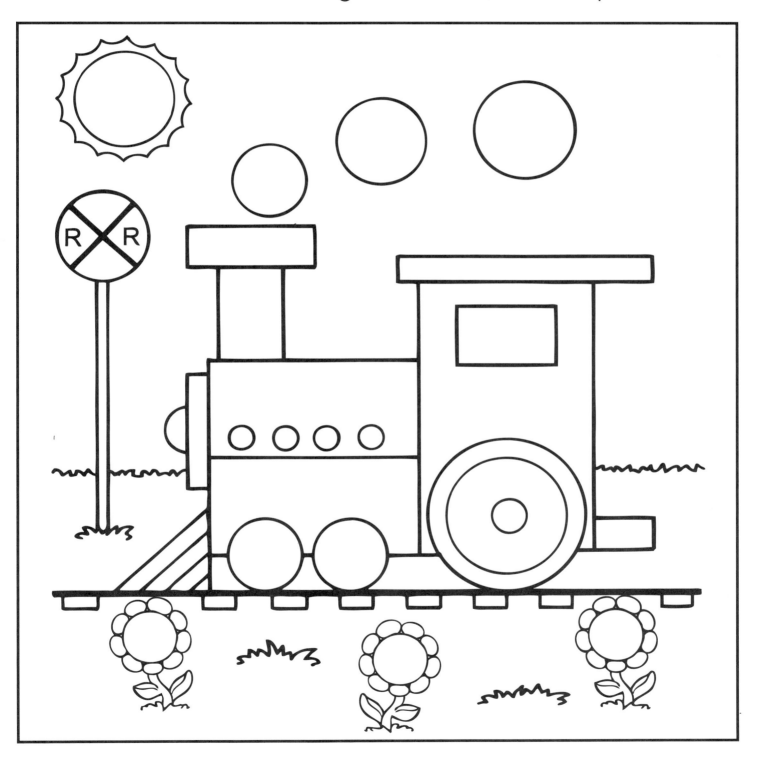

Copyright © 2010 by David A. Sousa. All rights reserved. Reprinted from *Brain-Compatible Activities for Mathematics, Grades K–1*, by David A. Sousa. Thousand Oaks, CA: Corwin, www.corwinpress.com. Reproduction authorized only for the local school site or nonprofit organization that has purchased this book.

3-D SHAPES

Objective

Students will identify three-dimensional shapes such as spheres, cones, cylinders, and cubes.

Anticipatory Set

Read aloud the book *Cubes, Cones, Cylinders, and Spheres* by Tana Hoban. Show students the shapes on the first page. Then ask them to look for the shapes in the pictures in the book.

Purpose

Tell students they will be able to identify three-dimensional shapes.

Input

Make several copies of the **3-D Shape Cards reproducible (page 82)** on heavy paper. Cut out the cards, and use a hole punch to punch two holes near the top corners of each card. String yarn through the holes in the cards, and tie the ends of the yarn together to create a necklace for each card. Make sure to prepare one shape necklace for each student.

Modeling

Place a shape necklace around your neck. Point to and identify the shape on the card for students. Explain that you will give them a direction, and they must listen carefully to see if they are supposed to follow the direction. For example, say, "Everyone who is wearing a cone necklace, reach your arms in the air." Then model how to reach your arms in the air. Explain, "I may also give clues such as, *If you are wearing the shape of an ice cream cone, stomp your feet*, or *If you are wearing the shape of a die, snap your fingers.*"

Checking for Understanding

Make sure that students know the name of each three-dimensional shape. Show one shape card at a time, and ask students to identify it.

Guided Practice

Give each student a shape card necklace to put on. Have students put their necklaces on with the shapes facing outward so everyone can see them. Then give directions for students to follow.

Examples

- If you have a cone, clap three times.
- If you are wearing the same shape as a ball, raise your hands.
- Everyone wearing a cube, touch your toes.

Closure

Encourage students to think about the three-dimensional shapes they studied. Ask them to think of two-dimensional shapes that are similar to three-dimensional shapes. For example, a square is similar to a cube, and a sphere is similar to a circle. Invite students to dictate, write, or draw in their math journals all the three-dimensional shapes they can think of at home or at school. For example, a cone can be a birthday party hat, an ice cream cone, or a megaphone. A cube can be an ice cube, a moving box, or a letter block.

Independent Practice

Invite students to make a class book titled *3-D Shapes Around Us.* Ask each student to draw a picture of a three-dimensional shape and then draw a picture of something in the environment that has the same shape. For example, if a student chooses a cylinder, he or she may draw a can of soup. If he or she chooses a sphere, that student may draw a soccer ball. Bind all students' pages together, and create a colorful cover. Place the book in the class library or math center for everyone to enjoy.

3-D Shape Cards

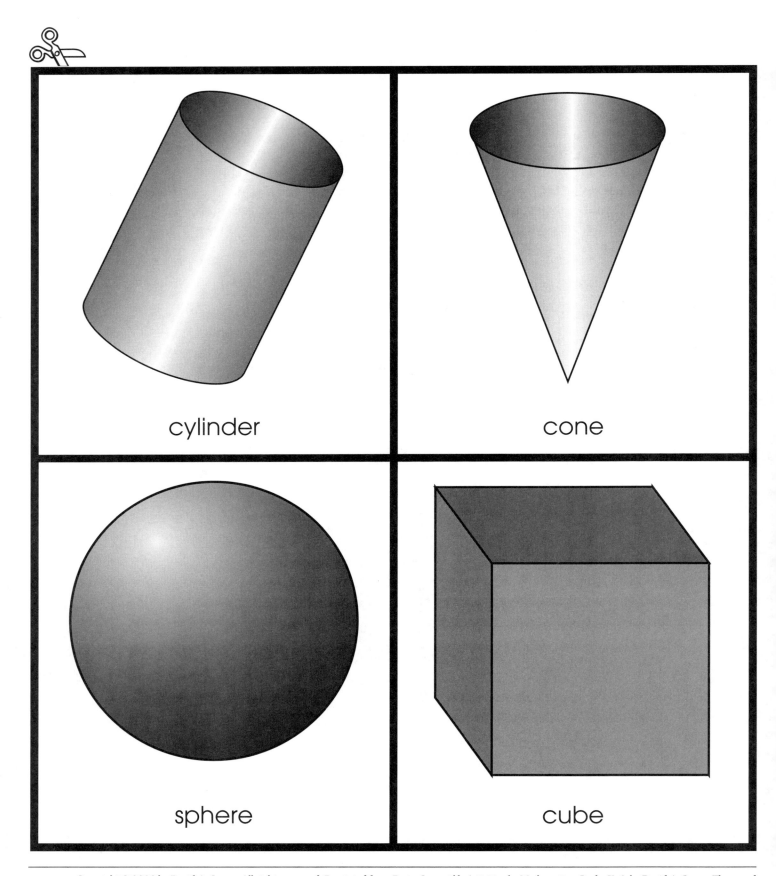

cylinder

cone

sphere

cube

82 Copyright © 2010 by David A. Sousa. All rights reserved. Reprinted from *Brain-Compatible Activities for Mathematics, Grades K–1*, by David A. Sousa. Thousand Oaks, CA: Corwin, www.corwinpress.com. Reproduction authorized only for the local school site or nonprofit organization that has purchased this book.

SHAPE UP

Objective

Students will create complex shapes using smaller, basic shapes.

Anticipatory Set

Read aloud the book *The Wing of a Flea* by Ed Emberley. Invite students to point out and identify the simple shapes. Discuss how the shapes are used to make other shapes and pictures of other items.

Purpose

Tell students that they will use some basic shapes to create a larger, more complex shape or a picture.

Input

Have pattern blocks available for students to use, or make several cutout shapes of triangles, squares, rectangles, trapezoids, and hexagons from colorful tagboard. Show the shapes to students, and ask them to name each one.

Modeling

Explain that we can create some shapes by putting together other, simpler shapes. On the overhead projector, model how to place four triangles together to create a larger triangle. Then assemble several shapes to create a design or a picture. For example, make a flower by placing a hexagon on the overhead, with one square touching each side. Or make a snowman by placing three circles in a vertical line and adding a rectangle and square for a top hat.

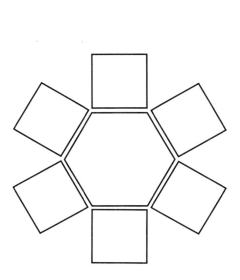
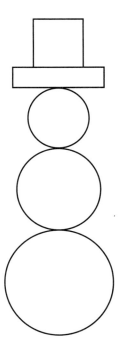

Checking for Understanding

Make sure that students understand that they are placing shapes next to each other to create larger shapes, designs, or pictures. Invite them to practice by making the hexagon flower you created during Modeling.

Guided Practice

Arrange the class into student pairs. Give each pair several pattern blocks or shape cutouts. Have one student create a complex shape using the pattern blocks. Then have his or her partner use the blocks to replicate the shape. Have partners switch roles.

Closure

Ask students to think about how they joined the shapes to make designs or pictures. Ask them if it is easier to match shapes that have straight sides or shapes such as circles and ovals. Invite them to share their responses with partners.

Independent Practice

Invite students to create shape designs and draw them in their math journals. If they have difficulty drawing their designs, have them trace the shape cutouts. Ask students to count the number of each type of shape they used in their designs and write it next to their pictures. Have students color their pictures using crayons or markers.

SHAPES EVERYWHERE

Objective

Students will identify shapes in the environment.

Anticipatory Set

Scatter various shape blocks or cutouts on the floor. Tell students that shapes are everywhere around them, in school, at home, around the community, and in nature. Play music, and have students walk around the shapes. Ask students to pick up a shape when the music stops. Then have each student identify his or her shape. Have students return their shapes to the floor and repeat the process. Tell them that later they will be looking for more shapes in the surrounding environment.

Purpose

Tell students they will look for shapes in their environment.

Input

Review shape names and characteristics with students. Name various shapes, and invite volunteers to draw them on the board.

Modeling

Walk around the classroom. Tell students that you see many shapes. Point to a table, and outline the shape with your finger. Say, "This is a rectangle." Point to the clock, outline the shape, and say, "This is a circle." Repeat the process with other objects in the classroom.

Checking for Understanding

Make sure that students are familiar with shapes and the way they look. Draw shapes on the board, and have students identify them.

Guided Practice

Take the class outside, and walk around the playground and through the hallways. Have students look for shapes. Call on volunteers to point to different objects and name the shapes, for example, rectangle—door, circle—tetherball court, triangle—yield sign, square—window, and octagon—stop sign.

Return to the classroom, and give each student a piece of drawing paper and crayons. Have each student draw a picture of one shape object he or she saw on the walk. Tell each student also to draw a picture of the shape that matches his or her object. Ask students to label both the object and the shape.

Closure

Ask students to think of objects in their homes. Have them draw pictures of some of the objects and identify their shapes in their math journals, for example, rectangle—refrigerator, bed, desktop, dining room table, placemat, coffee table; square—television, computer monitor, washcloth; oval—mirror, sink; circle—plate, clock, dog dish. You may wish to have students complete this as a homework activity.

Independent Practice

Give students copies of **The Same Shape reproducible (page 87)**. Tell students that they will draw a picture of an object that is the shape of a circle, one that is the shape of a square, one that is the shape of a triangle, and one that is the shape of a rectangle. Have them label each picture.

Name_____   Date_____

The Same Shape

Directions: Draw a picture of an object for each shape.

Circle ◯	Square ☐
This is a _____.	This is a _____.
Triangle △	Rectangle ▭
This is a _____.	This is a _____.

Copyright © 2010 by David A. Sousa. All rights reserved. Reprinted from *Brain-Compatible Activities for Mathematics, Grades K–1*, by David A. Sousa. Thousand Oaks, CA: Corwin, www.corwinpress.com. Reproduction authorized only for the local school site or nonprofit organization that has purchased this book.

THE ART OF SHAPES!

Objective

Integrating art, students will compose and decompose plane and solid figures.

Anticipatory Set

Get students' attention by dressing up as Captain Super Shape. Tape or pin colorful paper shapes on your shirt, and wear a long cape. Place a cone-shaped hat on your head. "Fly" around the room "rescuing" all the shapes found in the classroom. Pick up the rectangular poster board, the spherical ball, the cylinder-shaped soda can, or anything else you can find. Encourage students to help you rescue the shapes!

Purpose

Tell students that they are going to learn about plane and solid figures by creating shape art.

Input

Before the activity, locate pictures or manipulatives of various geometric shapes. Hold up the shapes. Discuss the names and attributes of each plane and solid figure.

Talk about how some shapes fit together to create other shapes (*two squares make a rectangle*) and other shapes change when taken apart (*a square becomes two triangles*).

1. Display a large sheet of paper in the shape of a rectangle. Ask students to name and describe this shape. Point out that this is a two-dimensional shape called a plane.

2. Cut the rectangle in half to create two squares. Discuss the characteristics of squares, pointing out that they too are planes.

3. Take one square, and cut it in half to create two triangles. Discuss the characteristics of the triangles.

4. Then use a large sheet of paper to model how to glue the shapes back together. For example, glue the two triangles together to make a square. Discuss this part-whole relationship.

5. Last, display several solid figured shapes such as a cereal box or a paper towel roll. Cut them apart to demonstrate how to decompose solid figures, emphasizing the part-whole relationship.

Modeling

Show students a piece of shape art that you have created. It can be anything that you have made using various shapes. Talk about how you created your shape art, and use correct terminology when referring to plane and solid figures. "I started with a large Styrofoam sphere. Then I glued a cone to the top for a hat. I cut out circles for the eyes and a triangle for the nose. The mouth is an oval. I glued all the paper shapes to the sphere."

Guided Practice

Prior to the lesson, create a shape art center. Cut out a wide variety of plane and solid figures from colored construction paper. Provide an assortment of solid figures such as Styrofoam balls or cones, paper towel rolls, soda cans, or gift boxes. Label the plane and solid figures, and set them in two different areas of the center. The center should also have art supplies available—glue, tape, scissors, yarn, markers, and crayons.

Invite students to the center to create their own shape art. They can use any of the plane or solid figures to create any piece of art they desire. Encourage creativity, and play lively music (no lyrics) while students work. Remind them to think and say aloud the names of the figures as they select them.

Closure

After everyone has visited the center, invite students to share their masterpieces with the class. Encourage them to explain what they did using the correct terminology for plane and solid figures. Applaud all efforts and creativity.

Ask students to write about the experience. Remind them to use correct terminology and attributes when describing their work.

SMART SHAPES

Objective

Students will be able to recognize and describe attributes of two-dimensional shapes and three-dimensional shapes.

Anticipatory Set

Hold an object behind your back. Describe the characteristics of the object. Based on your description, ask students to guess what object you are holding behind your back. Once the object is guessed, ask students to share additional details that could be used to describe the object.

Purpose

Tell students that they are going describe two-dimensional and three-dimensional shapes. They will do this playing a fun card game.

Input

Before playing the game, assess students' level of understanding of two-dimensional and three-dimensional shapes. Display pictures of two-dimensional shapes such as triangles, rectangles, squares, circles, and ovals. Review their names and the number of sides and faces on each shape. Compare the shapes with each other.

Modeling

Before the lesson, copy the **Smart Shapes Game Cards reproducibles (pages 92–93)** onto cardstock. Cut out and laminate them for durability. Make one set for every two students.

Partner students. Distribute a set of games cards to each team, and model how to play the game.

1. Shuffle the cards, and give each player five cards.

2. The first player chooses one of his or her own cards and describes the figure without saying the name (*the figure has three sides*).

3. The second player must identify the figure based on clues given by player 1. If player 2 can guess correctly, he or she gets to keep the card.

4. The player with the most cards in his or her pile wins the game.

Checking for Understanding

Ask a volunteer to explain how the game is played. Clarify any misunderstandings.

Guided Practice

Tell students that they may choose a place in the classroom to play the smart shapes game with their partners. Give students sufficient time to complete one game. Circulate around the room, guiding students in the rules and accuracy of game play.

Closure

Using a set of Smart Shapes cards, ask volunteers to play a round with you. Give the class an opportunity to talk about how they played with their partners, strategies they used, or things they learned.

Independent Practice

Ask students to complete the **Smart Shape Riddles reproducible (page 94)** for homework.

> Practice should be limited to the smallest amount of material or skill that has the most relevancy for the students.

Smart Shapes Game Cards

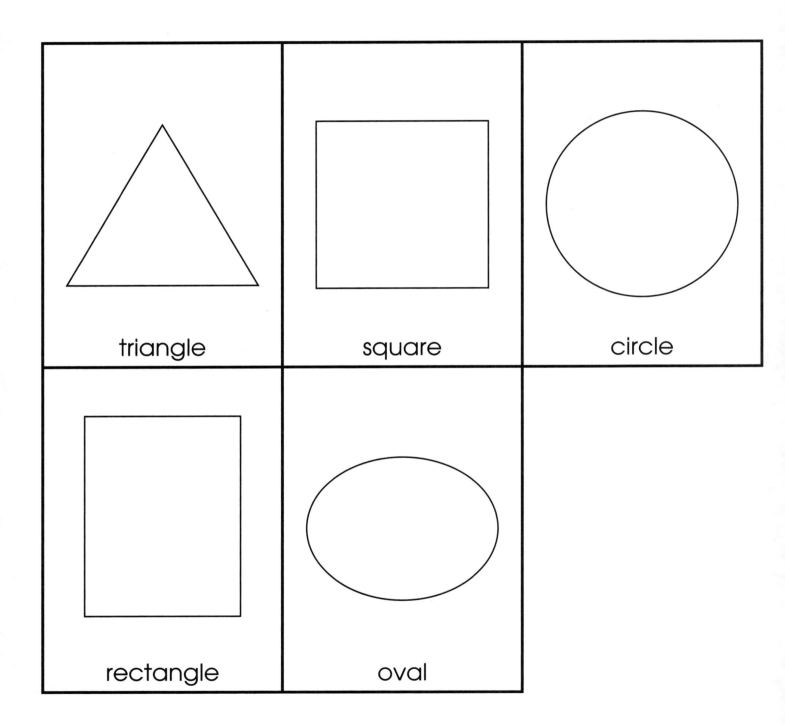

triangle

square

circle

rectangle

oval

92 Copyright © 2010 by David A. Sousa. All rights reserved. Reprinted from *Brain-Compatible Activities for Mathematics, Grades K–1*, by David A. Sousa. Thousand Oaks, CA: Corwin, www.corwinpress.com. Reproduction authorized only for the local school site or nonprofit organization that has purchased this book.

Smart Shapes Game Cards

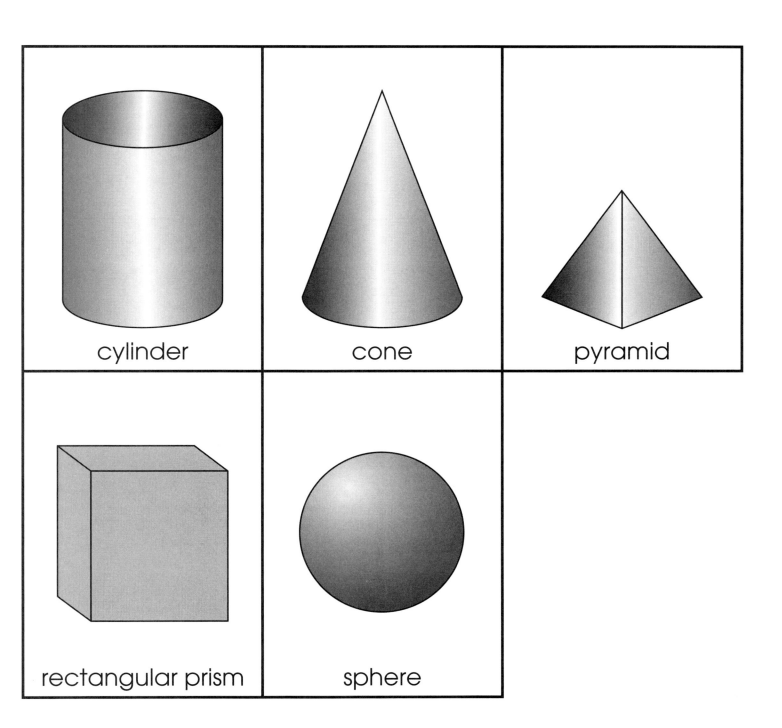

cylinder

cone

pyramid

rectangular prism

sphere

Copyright © 2010 by David A. Sousa. All rights reserved. Reprinted from *Brain-Compatible Activities for Mathematics, Grades K–1*, by David A. Sousa. Thousand Oaks, CA: Corwin, www.corwinpress.com. Reproduction authorized only for the local school site or nonprofit organization that has purchased this book.

Name_____   Date_____

Smart Shape Riddles

Directions: Circle the correct answer.

1. I have three sides. What am I?

   triangle   square

2. I am 3-dimensional with no sides or points. What am I?

   cone    sphere

3. I have four equal sides. What am I?

   square   rectangle

Directions: Draw 3 of your favorite shapes.

94 Copyright © 2010 by David A. Sousa. All rights reserved. Reprinted from *Brain-Compatible Activities for Mathematics, Grades K–1*, by David A. Sousa. Thousand Oaks, CA: Corwin, www.corwinpress.com. Reproduction authorized only for the local school site or nonprofit organization that has purchased this book.

THE SHAPE MUSEUM

Objective

Students will recognize shapes from different perspectives and orientations.

Anticipatory Set

Ask students to recall a trip to a museum. Invite volunteers to describe their experiences. Ask students who haven't visited a museum to think about displays they have seen around school, at the library, or in stores.

Purpose

Tell students that they are going to learn about different shapes by creating a shape museum.

Input

Display three cylinders, such as a candle, a drum, and a soup can. Ask students to describe the objects. Pose questions about these objects' similarities and differences. Invite students to come forward and examine the three objects.

> Providing students the opportunity to communicate their actions can clarify mathematical terms and phrases.

Show pictures or manipulatives of other three-dimensional shapes such as cylinders, pyramids, rectangular prisms, spheres, and cones. Hold up each figure while you say its correct name. Have students repeat the names of the shapes after you. Then encourage students to describe the attributes of these objects.

Before starting the activity, pose questions to see if students understand the concept of shapes' having different perspectives and orientations. Use the objects that you have collected to compare and contrast. Hold up two objects, and call on different students to offer their observations.

Modeling

Explain to students that you want to turn the classroom into a shape museum. Designate various parts of the room for your museum. Label these areas using the **Three-Dimensional Shape Labels reproducible (page 97).**

> Whenever possible, connect concepts to the real world to create purpose and meaning.

Model how to place various objects in the designated areas of the room. Place a ball in the sphere exhibit. Place a book in the rectangular prism exhibit. Explain to students why these objects belong in these exhibits and not in others. If possible use three-dimensional geometric models of a sphere and rectangular prism to compare and discuss similarities. Brainstorm other objects that might be placed in the different shape exhibits. Record student responses on the board. Read the list to students, and discuss how three-dimensional shapes are all around us.

Checking for Understanding

Ask students to raise their right hands if they think they understand what to do and raise their left hands if they need more explanation.

Guided Practice

Transfer the brainstorm list of objects to a letter to send home. Ask students to bring back to class one object from the list for the shape museum. Help students place the items in the correct locations.

Explain that they are going to visit the shape museum. Discuss the museum rules. Distribute the **Shape Museum Notes reproducible (page 98).** Tell students that they can write or draw pictures about the different shapes in the museum. As students visit the different exhibits, guide them in examining the shapes and recording their observations.

Closure

Invite students to write in their math journals about the shape museum and what they learned. Use the journal prompts on page 179.

Three-Dimensional Shape Labels

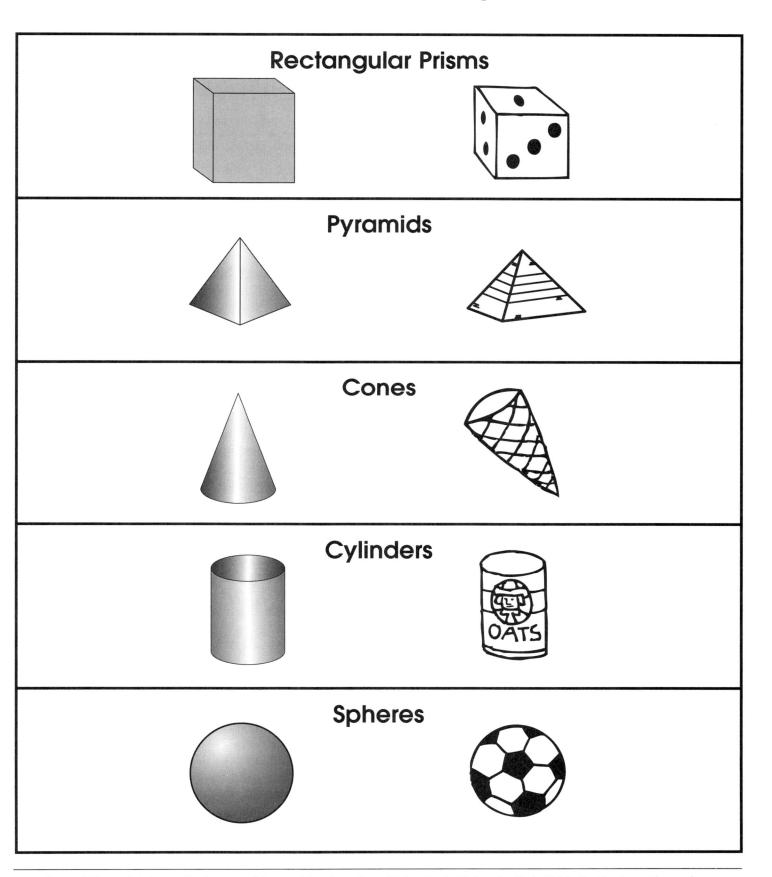

Rectangular Prisms

Pyramids

Cones

Cylinders

Spheres

Copyright © 2010 by David A. Sousa. All rights reserved. Reprinted from *Brain-Compatible Activities for Mathematics, Grades K–1*, by David A. Sousa. Thousand Oaks, CA: Corwin, www.corwinpress.com. Reproduction authorized only for the local school site or nonprofit organization that has purchased this book.

Name_____ **Date**_____

Shape Museum Notes

Directions: Draw pictures or write about the Shape Museum.

rectangular prisms
pyramids 
cones 
cylinders
spheres

98 Copyright © 2010 by David A. Sousa. All rights reserved. Reprinted from *Brain-Compatible Activities for Mathematics, Grades K–1*, by David A. Sousa. Thousand Oaks, CA: Corwin, www.corwinpress.com. Reproduction authorized only for the local school site or nonprofit organization that has purchased this book.

4

Measurement

WHICH IS LONGER?

Objective

Students will directly compare the lengths of two objects.

Anticipatory Set

Show two unsharpened pencils. Place them side by side. Explain that they are the same length. Then ask two students to stand side by side. Explain that you are comparing their heights, or how long they are. Ask students to tell you who is taller, or longer.

Purpose

Tell students that they will compare the lengths of objects.

Input

Cut various lengths of ribbon, and place the ribbon pieces in a basket. Tell students that when they compare two objects, they must place them side by side and align one end of each object. Draw two lines on the board to demonstrate. Make one line longer than the other, and point out that one end of each object aligns. Explain that this is how to compare the length of these two lines. This way, it is easy to see which one is longer than the other.

Modeling

Pull two ribbons from the basket, and hold them up so all students can see. Explain how you are holding one end of each ribbon and are placing those ends side by side so you can compare the length of the ribbons. Ask a volunteer to identify which ribbon is longer. Then tell students that you want to find a ribbon that is shorter than these two ribbons. Pull a shorter ribbon from the basket, and compare it to the other two ribbons by holding them side by side. Ask a volunteer to identify which ribbon is longest and which ribbon is shortest.

Checking for Understanding

Make sure students understand what the terms *longer* and *shorter* mean. Ask several volunteers to compare the length of two items in the classroom, such as two pencils, two pieces of chalk, two shoes, or two markers.

Guided Practice

Give each student a piece of ribbon from the basket. Tell students that they are going to walk around the room and compare their ribbon with other students' ribbons. Direct them to say whether their ribbon is shorter or longer than their classmates' ribbons.

Then gather the group together. Ask one student to stand and show his or her ribbon. Ask students who think they have shorter ribbons to stomp their feet. Then ask students who think they have longer ribbons to clap their hands. Repeat several times to make sure students grasp the concepts of shorter and longer.

Closure

Ask students to name one important thing to do when they are comparing the length of two objects (*Line up one end of each object.*). Have them discuss with partners why that is important. Then have them draw two objects or simple shapes in their math journals, one longer than the other. Ask them to identify which object is shorter and which object is longer.

Independent Practice

Give each student a copy of the **Comparing Lengths reproducible (page 102)** and a ruler. Tell students that they will walk around the classroom to find one thing that is shorter than the ruler, one that is the same size as the ruler, and one that is longer than the ruler. Direct them to draw and label on the reproducible a picture of each object they find.

Comparing Lengths

Directions: Draw an object that is shorter than a ruler. Draw an object that is the same size as a ruler. Draw an object that is longer than a ruler. Then finish each sentence.

_____ is shorter than the ruler.

_____ is the same size as the ruler.

_____ is longer than the ruler.

102 Copyright © 2010 by David A. Sousa. All rights reserved. Reprinted from *Brain-Compatible Activities for Mathematics, Grades K–1*, by David A. Sousa. Thousand Oaks, CA: Corwin, www.corwinpress.com. Reproduction authorized only for the local school site or nonprofit organization that has purchased this book.

MEASURE IT!

Objective

Students will use nonstandard measuring tools to compare the lengths of two objects.

Anticipatory Set

Point to a window in the classroom, and then point to a desk on the other side of the room. Tell students that you think the window is longer than the desk, but it is hard to tell because the objects are far away from each other. Explain that you cannot move the window to be near the desk, and you cannot lift the desk to be near the window, so it is difficult to compare their lengths.

Purpose

Tell students that they are going to work with partners to measure objects.

Input

Remind students that when they measure objects, they must line up the end of the measuring tool with one end of the object being measured.

Modeling

Model how to use Unifix cubes to measure the window. Write the window's measurement (number of cubes long) on the board. Repeat these steps for the desk. Compare the lengths, and say which one is longer. Explain that students will be using nonstandard units of measure rather than a ruler to measure objects. The cubes you used are considered nonstandard units of measure.

Checking for Understanding

Make sure partners understand that they have to measure each object from end to end. Have students demonstrate how to use the cubes to measure something. Make sure they are joining the cubes together to create a long stick.

Guided Practice

Organize students into pairs. Have each pair choose two objects to measure. Have the students draw a picture of the items on a piece of drawing paper. Then ask them to use Unifix cubes to measure the first object. Have them count the number of cubes for the length and write that number under their illustration. Then ask them to repeat the procedure for the second item. Ask students which object is longer.

Closure

Ask students how the measurement might change if they used pretzel sticks, large paperclips, or straws to measure the objects instead of Unifix cubes. Accept all reasonable responses. Demonstrate by inviting a volunteer to use one of these measuring tools to measure a shoe or a book. Then have him or her measure the same object using Unifix cubes. Ask students how the measurement changed. Reinforce the importance of using the same measuring tool to measure objects you are going to compare.

Then ask students to reflect on the activity in their math journals. Invite them to write or dictate one sentence that tells the most important thing they learned.

Independent Practice

Give each student a copy of the **Measure It! reproducible (page 105).** Direct students to choose four objects to measure. Have them draw a picture of each object. Then tell them to use Unifix cubes to measure the objects. Have them write the length of the objects by recording the number of cubes used.

Name_____   Date_____

Measure It!

Directions: Measure each object. Then draw the object and finish the sentence.

_____ is

_____ cubes long.

_____ is

_____ cubes long.

_____ is

_____ cubes long.

_____ is

_____ cubes long.

Copyright © 2010 by David A. Sousa. All rights reserved. Reprinted from *Brain-Compatible Activities for Mathematics, Grades K–1*, by David A. Sousa. Thousand Oaks, CA: Corwin, www.corwinpress.com. Reproduction authorized only for the local school site or nonprofit organization that has purchased this book.

ORDERING LENGTHS

Objective

Students will compare the lengths of objects and then order them.

Anticipatory Set

Tell students that often we place items in a certain order. Ordering items helps us to keep things organized or easier to find. Provide students with several simple examples. Explain that in a dictionary, the words are listed in alphabetical order. That means they are in order from *a* to *z*. Sometimes we are asked to stand in line in order from shortest to tallest. Ask students if they can think of any other ways that we order things in our lives.

Purpose

Tell students that they will compare the lengths of yarn and place the yarn pieces in order from shortest to longest.

Input

Tell students that when they compare lengths, they must line up the objects side by side and make sure that one end of one object is aligned with one end of the other object. Point out that the comparison will be incorrect if the objects are not lined up side by side.

Modeling

Gather five pencils of varying lengths. Show the pencils to students. Explain that the pencils are of different lengths because some have been sharpened and used more than others. Hold up two of the pencils, and place them side by side on the overhead projector. The opaque images created will provide students with a good example for comparison. Explain that you are lining up one end of each pencil (the eraser end) so you can compare the lengths. Point out the pencil that is longer. Then line up all the pencils. Model how to place them in order from shortest to longest.

Checking for Understanding

Make sure students understand the concept of shorter and longer. Show two items and have students identify which is shorter and which is longer.

Guided Practice

Cut pieces of yarn into various lengths. Organize students into pairs, and give each pair five pieces of yarn. Tell students to compare the lengths of their yarn pieces and then place them in order from shortest to longest. As students work, circulate around the classroom making sure students stay on task and understand the activity. Remind them that they must line up one end of each yarn piece to get an accurate comparison.

After students are finished ordering their yarn pieces, have one student in each pair hold up their longest piece of yarn. Have the pair of students stand together at the front of the room and compare their yarn pieces. Ask the rest of the class which yarn piece is the longest.

Closure

Ask students to stand in a line. Direct them to organize themselves in order from shortest to tallest. Ask a volunteer to check the line to make sure that students are in the correct order. If some students are out of order, encourage the volunteer to place those students in the correct places in line.

Invite students to write or dictate one or two sentences in their math journals describing one important thing they learned during the activity.

Independent Practice

Give students five paper strips of various lengths. Have them glue the strips on a piece of paper in order from shortest to longest.

HOW FAR?

Objective

Students will use nonstandard measuring tools to measure distance.

Anticipatory Set

Ask a volunteer to remove one of his or her shoes. Show students the shoe, and say, "[Student's name]'s foot is this long." Ask another student to take off his or her shoe. Show the class this shoe as well, and explain that this student's foot is as long as the shoe.

Purpose

Tell students that they are going to measure distance (how far something is) using the size of their shoes.

Input

Explain to students that they will be measuring distance using their shoes. They will need to place their shoes in a line, one in front of the other, when they are measuring.

Checking for Understanding

Make sure students understand that when they measure, they need to line up the shoes from back to front. Have them practice placing a shoe on the floor and then placing another one in front of it so that its heel is touching the toe of the first shoe.

Modeling

Tell students that they are going to measure the distance from one object in the room to another object. Explain that they will use their shoes to measure the distance. Because their shoes are shorter than the distance they will measure, they must use their shoes several times.

Model lining up the heel of one shoe with the starting point of the distance you are measuring. Then place the heel of your other shoe against the front end of the first shoe. Continue by lifting the first shoe and placing the heel next to the front of the other shoe. Each time you place a shoe, draw a tally mark on the board to keep track of the number of shoe lengths you use.

Guided Practice

Divide the class into student pairs. Have one partner take off both of his or her shoes to use for measuring. Tell students to pick two locations in the room, such as the teacher's desk and the door, to measure. Then have partners use the shoes to measure the distance between the two locations.

Tell students that one partner should place the shoes while the other partner keeps track of the number of shoe lengths used. Students can count to keep track or draw tally marks on a piece of scrap paper.

Closure

Ask students to think about the following question: How could two students who measured the same distance from the teacher's desk to the classroom door get different measurements? Invite them to discuss their ideas with their partners. Then ask them to write or dictate a response to this question in their math journals.

Independent Practice

Give students a copy of the **How Far? reproducible (page 110).** Tell students that they will use their shoes to measure the distance between two objects or locations in the classroom. Have students draw a picture of both objects in the frames provided. Then have them complete the sentence frame.

Name _____ Date _____

How Far?

Directions: Use your 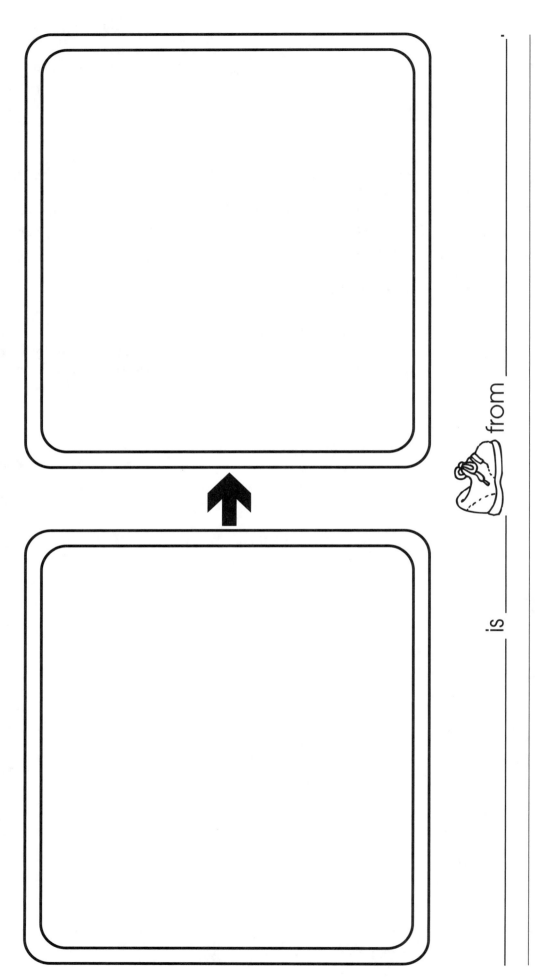 to measure the distance between two objects. Draw a picture of each object. Then finish the sentence.

_____ is _____ from _____.

Copyright © 2010 by David A. Sousa. All rights reserved. Reprinted from *Brain-Compatible Activities for Mathematics, Grades K–1*, by David A. Sousa. Thousand Oaks, CA: Corwin, www.corwinpress.com. Reproduction authorized only for the local school site or nonprofit organization that has purchased this book.

WHICH HOLDS MORE?

Objective

Students will compare the capacity of two containers.

Anticipatory Set

Show students several jars of different sizes. Explain that these containers can hold liquids (such as orange juice or water) or solid objects (such as pennies or jellybeans). Line up the jars from shortest to tallest.

Purpose

Tell students they will measure how much (the capacity) two jars can hold.

Input

Divide the class into small groups. Tell students that they will measure how many cups of rice can fit in each of two jars and then compare how much each jar can hold. Give each group a tub filled with uncooked rice, a measuring cup, and two different-sized jars labeled "1" and "2." Tell students that they must carefully fill the measuring cup over the tub so rice does not spill on the floor.

Modeling

Model how to use the measuring cup to scoop up the rice and pour it into a jar. Show students how to fill the measuring cup to the top and level it off with the side of your hand. Tell students that if you do not fill the cup each time, your measurement will not be accurate. Invite students to count along with you as you scoop up each cup and pour it into the jar until the jar is full. Then ask students to tell you the final measurement.

Checking for Understanding

Have students scoop out rice with a measuring cup to check that they completely fill the cup and level it off with the sides of their hands. Assist students as needed.

Guided Practice

Before beginning the activity, ask students to predict which of their two jars will hold more rice, jar 1 or jar 2. Then ask them to use the measuring cup to fill each jar. Direct them to have one group member draw a tally mark each time they pour a cup of rice into a jar. When they are done filling each jar, ask students to count the tally marks to see which jar held more rice.

Closure

Writing can be an effective assessment tool for both students and teachers.

Ask students, "Which jar did you think would hold more rice? Why did you think that? Were you correct? What did you learn by doing this activity?" Invite them to dictate or write their responses in their math journals.

Independent Practice

Place a variety of different-sized containers, such as small boxes, jars, bowls, cups, empty milk cartons, and so on, in the math center. (Make sure all containers have whole-number capacities, such as one cup, two cups, or five cups. Students are not yet prepared to work with fractional capacities.) Label each container with a number. Place a tub of rice and a measuring cup in the center as well.

Give each student a copy of the **Fill It Up reproducible (page 113)** to complete with a partner. Invite pairs to take turns visiting the math center to complete the reproducible activity. First, have students choose two containers. Then have them use the measuring cup to fill the containers with rice to see which one holds more. Then have them answer the questions on the reproducible.

Name _____ Date _____

Fill It Up

Directions: Draw a picture of each container. Measure rice into each one. Then answer the question.

Container 1 holds _____ cups.

Container 2 holds _____ cups.

Which container holds more rice? _____

Copyright © 2010 by David A. Sousa. All rights reserved. Reprinted from *Brain-Compatible Activities for Mathematics, Grades K–1*, by David A. Sousa. Thousand Oaks, CA: Corwin, www.corwinpress.com. Reproduction authorized only for the local school site or nonprofit organization that has purchased this book.

HOW LONG? MEASURING WITH TENS AND ONES

Objective

Students will use ones-blocks and tens-blocks to measure objects.

Anticipatory Set

Choose two or three students to bring forward items to measure (e.g., a pencil or a book). Talk about the length of each object, and pose questions that create conversation about measurement.

Purpose

Tell students that they are going to practice measuring objects using ones-blocks and tens-blocks. Suggest that this activity will also help them learn to record and organize information.

Input

Display 10 ones-blocks and 1 tens-block. Remind students that the tens-block is the same size as 10 of the ones-blocks. If necessary, place 10 ones-blocks adjacent to each other and compare the length to that of the tens-block.

Modeling

Teach the new material first, during prime time.

Model how to measure an object (such as a book) using ones-blocks. Demonstrate how to carefully line up the ones-blocks to produce an accurate measurement. Measure the same item using tens-blocks. If the measurement is not exact, explain how ones-blocks can be used to complete the measurement. Think aloud, and record your answers on the board: "The book is 25 ones-blocks long. As I use my tens-blocks, I can see that the book is 2 tens-blocks long, with some space left over. I will use ones-blocks to complete the measurement. The book is 2 tens-blocks and 5 ones-blocks long. I know that 2 tens is equal to 20, plus 5 ones, which equals 25."

Checking for Understanding

Assess understanding by orally questioning students about ones-blocks and tens-blocks. Repeat examples as needed.

Guided Practice

Distribute ones-blocks and tens-blocks. Tell students that they are going to measure various objects from the classroom. Distribute a copy of the **Record Sheet reproducible (page 116)** to each student. Consider allowing students to work in pairs or small groups. Tell students to select five items to measure and to record the names of the items on their record sheets. Prompt them to measure the objects, using tens-blocks and/or ones-blocks, and then record the lengths on the reproducible. Circulate around the room, and assist as needed.

Closure

Instruct each student to partner with another student to share and compare record sheets. Do students see similarities and differences? Are there objects that they would like to go back and remeasure? If so, allow them the necessary time to do so. In addition, invite students to use this time to continue measuring and recording objects within the classroom.

Prompt students to think about what they learned by writing in their math journals. Ask questions such as, *How many ones-blocks equal a tens-block? If an item is 13 ones-blocks long, how many tens-blocks are needed? How many ones?* and *How might using tens-blocks and ones-blocks help you in other areas of math?*

Name_____ Date_____

Record Sheet

Directions: Use ones-blocks and tens-blocks to measure the lengths of objects. Record the lengths below.

Item	Length		
	Tens	Ones	Total

116 Copyright © 2010 by David A. Sousa. All rights reserved. Reprinted from *Brain-Compatible Activities for Mathematics, Grades K–1*, by David A. Sousa. Thousand Oaks, CA: Corwin, www.corwinpress.com. Reproduction authorized only for the local school site or nonprofit organization that has purchased this book.

GOING ON A MEASUREMENT HUNT

Objective

Students will use nonstandard units of measure to find the length of various objects.

Anticipatory Set

Gain class attention by telling one student to lie on the floor. Using miniature candy bars, measure the length of this student from head to toe. Repeat with another student whose length differs from that of the first one. Discuss the lengths of both students.

Purpose

Tell students they are going to use nonstandard units of measure to go on a measurement hunt in the classroom.

Input

Talk about why we need to measure things and some of the instruments we use to do that. Explain why we sometimes use objects other than rulers to measure length. Introduce the idea that smaller units of measurement (such as an eraser) will result in a larger number of units needed. A larger unit of measurement (such as a pencil case) will result in fewer units needed. Discuss the use of words such as *about, almost, long,* and *length* when using nonstandard units of measure.

Make sure students understand that because they are using a nonstandard unit of measure, their answers may not be exact but may be an estimate (an object is about 5 paperclips long).

Modeling

Show students how to measure the length of the chalkboard using several copies of the same textbook. Write the answer on the board. Be sure to use terms such as *about, long,* and *length.* Ask a volunteer to use the textbook to measure the length of the teacher's desk and record the measurement on the board. Repeat this activity, asking volunteers to choose a different nonstandard unit of measure (other than a book) to measure the desk. Record the measurement on the board. Think aloud as you make a comparison of different units of measure: "The desk is about 6 textbooks long, but it is 22 pencils long. Because the pencil is shorter than the textbook, it takes more pencils to measure the same length."

Checking for Understanding

Use the thumbs-up or thumbs-down strategy to check for understanding.

Guided Practice

Provide each student with a paper clip and a pencil. Distribute the **Classroom Measurement Hunt reproducible (page 119).** Tell students that they must find various objects around the room that are the same length as the measurements listed on the reproducible. Students will write the name of the object next to each measurement. If necessary, encourage students to collaborate on this step.

Closure

Have students respond to the journal questions from page 179. Have a brief class discussion about the usefulness of nonstandard units of measure.

Independent Practice

Give each student a copy of the **Home Measurement Hunt reproducible (page 120)** to complete for homework.

Name_____ Date_____

 # Classroom Measurement Hunt

Directions: List objects in the classroom that have the length and height of each of the following measurements.

Measurement	Item
3 paper clips long	
5 pencils long	
1 shoe long	
2 of your hands high	
As high as your neck	
As long as your arm	
As long as your favorite book	
As high as your leg	

Copyright © 2010 by David A. Sousa. All rights reserved. Reprinted from *Brain-Compatible Activities for Mathematics, Grades K–1*, by David A. Sousa. Thousand Oaks, CA: Corwin. www.corwinpress.com. Reproduction authorized only for the local school site or nonprofit organization that has purchased this book.
119

Name_____   Date_____

 # Home Measurement Hunt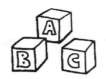

Directions: List objects at home that have the length and height of each of the following measurements.

Measurement	Item
3 spoons long	
5 shoes	
As long as your favorite toy	
2 of your hands high	
As high as your neck	
As long as your arm	
As long as your favorite book	
As high as your leg	

120 Copyright © 2010 by David A. Sousa. All rights reserved. Reprinted from *Brain-Compatible Activities for Mathematics, Grades K–1*, by David A. Sousa. Thousand Oaks, CA: Corwin, www.corwinpress.com. Reproduction authorized only for the local school site or nonprofit organization that has purchased this book.

COMPARISON CENTER

Objective

Students will compare length, weight, and volume.

Anticipatory Set

Write the words *tall*, *taller*, and *tallest* across the top of the chalkboard. Then invite three students to come forward. Organize those students according to height, asking them to stand under one of the three words. Discuss this comparison with your students.

Purpose

Tell students that they are going to work in a center to learn about comparing length, weight, and volume.

Input

Before students work in the center, brainstorm words that can be used to compare. Choose familiar words, including those listed below, and teach students any new terms. Ask students to make some comparisons of items or people with which they are already familiar. Lead the discussion by giving an example such as, *My car is heavier than my bicycle.*

Comparing Words

long, longer, longest

short, shorter, shortest

tall, taller, tallest

big, bigger, biggest

heavy, heavier, heaviest

full, fuller, fullest

Set up a comparison center for students to explore length, weight, and volume. Gather the following materials:

for comparing length—crayon, marker, paintbrush

for comparing volume—three clear plastic water bottles filled with different amounts of water and labeled "1," "2," and "3" with permanent marker

for comparing weight—marble, golf ball, tennis ball

Label the three stations "length," "volume," and "weight." Then place the items in the corresponding stations. Make class sets of the **Length, Volume,**

and Weight reproducibles (pages 123–125), and place them in the stations. Note that each reproducible may be cut in half and used for two students.

Modeling

Demonstrate how to make the comparisons in the center. Model how to examine each object and record the information on each reproducible. Think aloud as you work through each station in the center: "I am looking at the crayon, pencil, and paintbrush. I notice that the paintbrush is the longest item. It is longer than the pencil and longer than the crayon. But the pencil is longer than the crayon too. I will go to the reproducible and draw the crayon in the box labeled 'Long.'" Continue this way until students understand how to complete the activity.

Checking for Understanding

Invite a volunteer to explain what to do in the comparison center. Ask the rest of the students to raise their right hands if they understand what to do or raise their left hands if they need more explanation.

Guided Practice

Allow students to spend time in the comparison center individually or in small groups. Be available to assist if needed. Remind students to think about each item as they make a comparison and to record their observations on their reproducibles.

Closure

> Closure completes the rehearsal process and attaches sense and meaning to the new learning.

Invite students to write in their math journals about what they learned in the center. What objects did they compare? How will learning the terminology help them in other parts of math?

Name_____ Date_____

Length

Directions: Compare the objects, and show them below.

Long	
Longer	
Longest	

Name_____ Date_____

Length

Directions: Compare the objects, and show them below.

Long	
Longer	
Longest	

Copyright © 2010 by David A. Sousa. All rights reserved. Reprinted from *Brain-Compatible Activities for Mathematics, Grades K–1*, by David A. Sousa. Thousand Oaks, CA: Corwin, www.corwinpress.com. Reproduction authorized only for the local school site or nonprofit organization that has purchased this book.

Name_____ Date_____

Volume

Directions: Compare the water bottles, and show them below.

Full	Fuller	Fullest

Name_____ Date_____

Volume

Directions: Compare the water bottles, and show them below.

Full	Fuller	Fullest

124 Copyright © 2010 by David A. Sousa. All rights reserved. Reprinted from *Brain-Compatible Activities for Mathematics, Grades K–1*, by David A. Sousa. Thousand Oaks, CA: Corwin, www.corwinpress.com. Reproduction authorized only for the local school site or nonprofit organization that has purchased this book.

Name_____ Date_____

Weight

Directions: Compare the objects, and show them below.

Heavy	Heavier	Heaviest

Name_____ Date_____

Weight

Directions: Compare the objects, and show them below.

Heavy	Heavier	Heaviest

Copyright © 2010 by David A. Sousa. All rights reserved. Reprinted from *Brain-Compatible Activities for Mathematics, Grades K–1*, by David A. Sousa. Thousand Oaks, CA: Corwin, www.corwinpress.com. Reproduction authorized only for the local school site or nonprofit organization that has purchased this book.

TICK-TOCK AT THE CLOCK SHOP

Objective

Students will identify time to the nearest half hour.

Anticipatory Set

Gain class attention by reciting the words to the nursery rhyme "Hickory Dickory Dock." Start a discussion about clocks and time. Ask students what they do at various times of the day: "What do you do at 8:00 in the morning? What do you do at 12:30 on Saturday? What do you do at 5:00 at night?"

Purpose

Tell students that they are going to practice reading clocks to the nearest half hour by creating a classroom clock shop.

Input

Discuss why it is important that students know how to tell time. Provide students with the following times, displayed on a teaching clock: 3:00, 7:30, 11:00, and 2:30. Discuss the times. Emphasize the difference between the big hand and the little hand of the clock. Talk about what it means when the big hand is on the 12 and when it is on the 6.

Modeling

Using the **Clock Template reproducible (page 128),** a piece of construction paper, glue, scissors, and a brass fastener, demonstrate how to make a paper clock.

On the board, write "2:00." Ask students how they would change two o'clock to two thirty. Model 2:30 on the board. Make sure the students understand that they will be discussing time only to the nearest half hour. Therefore, remind students that the times will end only in *:00* and *:30*. Ask students to give some examples for you to demonstrate on the clock.

Guided Practice

Preadolescents are likely to respond emotionally to a learning situation much faster than rationally.

Distribute a copy of the Clock Template reproducible to each student. Guide students in assembling their own clocks. After the clocks are completed, provide students with construction paper to use to make their own individual clock frames. Students can glue the clocks to the construction paper and decorate the frames in any way they wish. Tell students to name their clocks and write the names on the construction paper below the faces (*Tran's Clock, The Cool Cuckoo Clock*). After the clocks are complete, give students an opportunity to practice setting their clocks at various times on the hour and on the half hour. Then tell students to set their clocks to a specific time of their choosing on the half hour and place their clocks faceup on their desktops. Next, have students line up outside the classroom in the hallway.

Once you are all outside, tell students to imagine that they are entering a clock shop. There are lots of clocks in this shop, and they are all set to different times. They will browse the clock shop and find four clocks they like. Then they will record the times of those clocks on their **Clock Shop reproducibles (page 129).** Distribute a copy of the Clock Shop reproducible to each student as he or she enters the room. As students shop for clocks and record the times, walk around the room assisting students who need help.

Closure

Ask students to refer to the Clock Shop reproducible as they write about their experience. Encourage them to think about what they did during the activity and what they learned about telling time to the half hour.

Independent Practice

Give each student a copy of the **Clock Shop Practice reproducible (page 130)** to complete individually. Explain that students will be writing the correct time under each clock in the shop.

Clock Template

128 Copyright © 2010 by David A. Sousa. All rights reserved. Reprinted from *Brain-Compatible Activities for Mathematics, Grades K–1*, by David A. Sousa. Thousand Oaks, CA: Corwin, www.corwinpress.com. Reproduction authorized only for the local school site or nonprofit organization that has purchased this book.

Name_____   Date_____

Clock Shop

Directions: Write the clock name on the line. Then draw the hands on the clock to show the time.

_____   _____

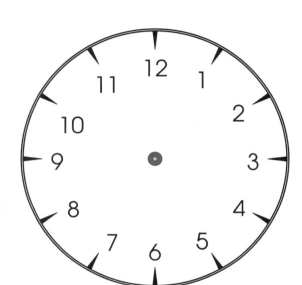   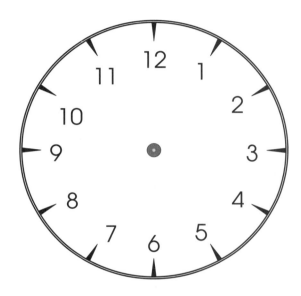

_____   _____

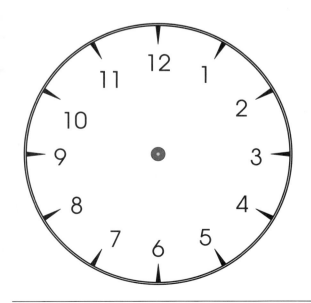   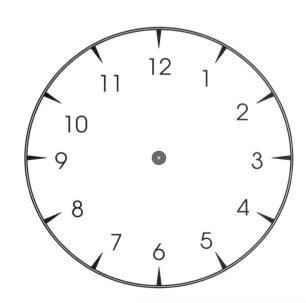

Copyright © 2010 by David A. Sousa. All rights reserved. Reprinted from *Brain-Compatible Activities for Mathematics, Grades K–1*, by David A. Sousa. Thousand Oaks, CA: Corwin, www.corwinpress.com. Reproduction authorized only for the local school site or nonprofit organization that has purchased this book.

Name_____   **Date**_____

Clock Shop Practice

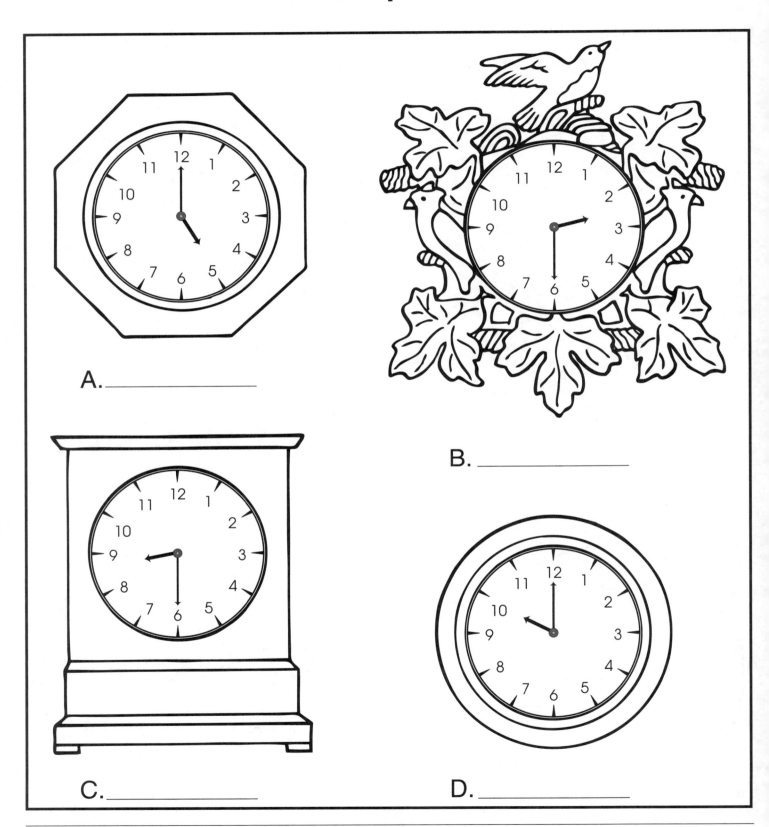

A._____

B._____

C._____

D._____

130 Copyright © 2010 by David A. Sousa. All rights reserved. Reprinted from *Brain-Compatible Activities for Mathematics, Grades K–1*, by David A. Sousa. Thousand Oaks, CA: Corwin, www.corwinpress.com. Reproduction authorized only for the local school site or nonprofit organization that has purchased this book.

BEFORE OR AFTER?

Objective

Students will relate time to real-life events by understanding the concepts before and after.

Anticipatory Set

Gain class attention by stating incorrect before and after examples: "Before I brush my teeth, I go to bed. I eat dessert before I eat lunch. After I eat dinner, I go to school." Pose questions that help students brainstorm the possible problems and confusion our world would have if everyone were confused about the meaning of *before* and *after.* Allow adequate wait time, and solicit oral responses.

Purpose

Tell students that they are going to learn about before and after.

Input

Students learn about the concept of before and after as they begin learning about describing measurement. Discuss how learning before and after will help them in telling time, measuring, using a number line, and many other things in real life. Give several examples using time: "We eat breakfast before we start school. Kevin goes to soccer practice after school." Try to include some other before and after examples using a number line or measurement tools.

Modeling

Before the lesson, prepare a list of 7 to 10 sentences relevant to your particular class or school. Use two-part sentences that include either *before* or *after:* "We do reading lessons before recess, and we have PE after lunch. We spread newspapers on the table before we work with clay, and we throw the newspapers in the recycling bin after we finish." Write the sentences on sentence strips, and place them in a pocket chart. Place a small blank card over the word *before* or *after* in each sentence.

Read the first sentence aloud without saying the word *before* or *after.* Ask a volunteer to fill in the missing word. Then remove the blank card to reveal the answer. Praise the student for the correct answer. Model a few other examples until students understand what to do.

Checking for Understanding

Use a thumbs-up or thumbs-down technique to check for understanding.

Guided Practice

Make a photocopy of the **Before and After Cards reproducible (page 133)** on cardstock for each student. Cut out and distribute one Before card and one After card to each student.

> Find out what students know and what their interests are, and use that information for motivation.

Read the sentences from the pocket chart aloud, omitting the hidden word. Ask students to hold up the card with the word that completes the sentence. Then reveal the answer by removing the blank card. Celebrate correct answers with a "Hooray!"

Closure

Ask students to glue the picture of a school (from page 133) into their math journals. Then ask them to draw something that they do before school and draw something that they do after school. Tell students to label their drawings "before" and "after." Challenge students to write a sentence about each of their pictures that uses the word *before* or *after.*

Ask students to think and write about the meaning of *before* and *after* and how knowing those terms will help them in other parts of math.

Independent Practice

Distribute the **Before I . . .** and **After I . . . reproducibles (pages 134–135)** to give students an opportunity to practice what they learned about before and after. Students should draw or write about something they do before or after each event shown on the reproducibles. Encourage group discussion about the events.

Before and After Cards

Before

After

Copyright © 2010 by David A. Sousa. All rights reserved. Reprinted from *Brain-Compatible Activities for Mathematics, Grades K–1*, by David A. Sousa. Thousand Oaks, CA: Corwin, www.corwinpress.com. Reproduction authorized only for the local school site or nonprofit organization that has purchased this book.

Name_____   Date_____

Before I . . .

Directions: Draw or write about something you do before each event.

Before

	Put on my shoes
	Go to sleep at night
	Eat my lunch
	Cross the street

134 Copyright © 2010 by David A. Sousa. All rights reserved. Reprinted from *Brain-Compatible Activities for Mathematics, Grades K–1,* by David A. Sousa. Thousand Oaks, CA: Corwin, www.corwinpress.com. Reproduction authorized only for the local school site or nonprofit organization that has purchased this book.

Name_____ Date_____

After I . . .

Directions: Draw or write about something you do after each event.

	After
Get up in the morning	
Take a bath	
Eat my lunch	
Play with my toys	

Copyright © 2010 by David A. Sousa. All rights reserved. Reprinted from *Brain-Compatible Activities for Mathematics, Grades K–1,* by David A. Sousa. Thousand Oaks, CA: Corwin, www.corwinpress.com. Reproduction authorized only for the local school site or nonprofit organization that has purchased this book.

Algebra

Sorting and Patterning

Number Patterns

What Comes Next?

Extending Patterns

Pattern Necklaces

Sorting Shoes

Sort and Classify

NUMBER PATTERNS

Objective

Students will create a number pattern.

Anticipatory Set

Before beginning the activity, make number necklaces for students. Write the numerals *1* through *20* on separate large index cards. Use a hole punch to make holes in the upper two corners of each card. String a piece of yarn through the holes, and tie the ends of the yarn together to make a necklace for each number.

Tell students that patterns are all around us. They can appear on the calendar and in many other places. Point out patterns found on student clothing. Then draw a series of shapes on the board or place a series of shape blocks along the chalk tray to form a pattern such as circle, circle, square, circle, circle, square. Point out the pattern. Then ask a volunteer to help you create another pattern for the class to guess.

Purpose

Tell students that they will look for number patterns.

Input

Ask students to look at the class calendar. Tell them that we can find number patterns on the calendar. Place small sticky notes on the even numbers on the calendar. Point to each even number, and say it aloud. Ask students to say the numbers aloud with you. Then remove the sticky notes, place them on every fifth number, and say them aloud: "5, 10, 15, 20, 25, 30." Point to each number again, and have students say the numbers aloud with you. Explain that these numbers follow a pattern.

> Mathematics can be defined simply as the science of patterns.

Modeling

Draw a number line on the board. Number it from 0 to 20. Then circle the numbers *2, 4, 6,* and *8.* Ask students which number they think should be circled next. Tell them to look at the numbers you circled. Explain, "If I look at the circled numbers, I notice that every other number is circled. So that means *9* would not be circled, but the next number, *10,* would be circled." Circle the number *10.*

Continue by circling other number patterns, such as multiples of three or five, in different colors. Ask students to identify the patterns.

Checking for Understanding

Make sure students understand that they are looking for a pattern, or what they see repeated. Write "1, 2, 3, 4" on the board, and ask students what would come next (5). Repeat with the numbers *7, 8, 9,* and *10.*

Guided Practice

Give each student a number necklace to wear. Have students wearing number cards 1, 2, and 3 stand at the front of the room. Then ask the student who is wearing the number that comes next in the pattern to stand next to student number 3. Repeat the activity with other number patterns.

Then ask students wearing number cards 2, 4, and 6 to stand at the front of the room. Ask the class which number comes next in this pattern. Have students refer to the number line that you drew on the board (see Modeling, above) if necessary. Repeat the activity with other counting-by-two number patterns.

Closure

Ask students to draw a number line in their math journals. Have them write the numbers *1* through *10.* Then ask them to circle numbers on the number line to show a number pattern. Check students' work to ensure that they understand the concept of number patterns.

Independent Practice

Give students a copy of the **Number Patterns reproducible (page 140).** Explain that they will look at each pattern and then continue the pattern by writing what comes next.

Number Patterns

Directions: Complete each number pattern.

A. 1, 2, 3, 4, 5, ____, ____, ____

B. 1, 2, 1, 2, 1, 2, ____, ____, ____

C. 10, 9, 8, 7, 6, 5, ____, ____, ____

D. 2, 4, 6, ____, ____, ____

E. 5, 6, 7, 8, ____, ____, ____

F. 1, 2, 3, 1, 2, 3, ____, ____, ____

G. 10, 8, 6, ____, ____, ____

H. 2, 5, 5, 2, 5, 5, ____, ____, ____

140 Copyright © 2010 by David A. Sousa. All rights reserved. Reprinted from *Brain-Compatible Activities for Mathematics, Grades K–1*, by David A. Sousa. Thousand Oaks, CA: Corwin, www.corwinpress.com. Reproduction authorized only for the local school site or nonprofit organization that has purchased this book.

WHAT COMES NEXT?

Objective

Students will identify sound patterns.

Anticipatory Set

Ask students to be quiet and close their eyes. Tell them to listen carefully for a sound. Ring a bell, and ask students to identify the sound. Then clap your hands, and ask them what sound they heard. Repeat with a variety of other sounds, such as recorded animal sounds or musical instruments like a recorder or a toy xylophone.

Purpose

Tell students they will listen and watch for patterns. Then they will continue the patterns.

Input

Show students some noisemakers such as a bell, maracas, or a triangle. Explain that each object makes a different sound. Ask students how they can make sounds using body parts (*clap hands, snap fingers, tap feet*).

Modeling

Tell students that they are going to listen for a pattern. Ring a bell, shake maracas, and clap your hands in a simple pattern. Repeat the pattern several times. Tell students, "The pattern I hear is bell, maracas, clap." Model a different pattern with three new sounds, such as snapping fingers, tapping a desk with a pencil, and stomping your feet.

Checking for Understanding

Check to see if students understand the concept of patterning. Write on the board, "AB AB," and ask students which letter comes next in the pattern. Allow students time to respond. Then repeat with the pattern ABC ABC.

Guided Practice

Ask students to sit at their desks and listen carefully for a pattern. Clap your hands and snap your fingers several times. Then have students join in by making the sounds along with you. Stop and ask, "Which comes next in the pattern, a clap or a snap?"

Repeat this procedure using other AB sound patterns. Then introduce ABC sound patterns. Make more complex patterns for more proficient students. If you feel students are ready, invite volunteers to come to the front of the room and create simple AB or ABC patterns for the class to guess. Provide them with objects to use to make the patterns, such as various classroom instruments, pencils or dowels, blocks, and more.

Closure

Ask students to describe what they learned about patterning. Have them write or dictate sentences in their math journals. Invite them to draw a picture of a pattern if they are having trouble describing it in words.

Independent Practice

Give each student a bag of Unifix cubes. Ask students to create patterns by joining the cubes together. Then have them exchange their cubes with partners to see if they can guess each other's patterns.

EXTENDING PATTERNS

Objective

Students will identify a pattern and then extend it.

Anticipatory Set

Before beginning the activity, create strips of tagboard or construction paper with patterns on them (sentence strips work well too). You can draw the objects, use shape cutouts, or use rubber stamps to create the patterns on the strips. Do not fill the entire strip, as students will be extending the patterns that you begin. Make sure you have one strip for each student.

Ask students if they have ever helped somebody complete a project or a task. Give students the first line to a story, such as, "Deep, deep down in the cold blue ocean. . . ." Then invite a volunteer to provide the next line to the story, such as, " . . . a big gray whale swam looking for food." Invite several volunteers to continue to contribute lines to the story.

Explain that when we work on something that someone else started, we need to look carefully at what that person did. As you created your story, each student's line had to build on what came before.

Purpose

Tell students that they will look at a pattern to identify it. Then they will continue the pattern.

Input

Use the overhead projector and overhead shapes or shape cutouts to create a variety of patterns. For example, two triangles, two squares, two triangles, two squares. Point out the AB AB pattern you created. Repeat with a few more patterns. Invite volunteers to identify the patterns.

Modeling

Hold up one of the sentence strips. Point out the pattern, and ask students to tell you what comes next in the pattern to keep it going. Use a rubber stamp or a marker to continue the pattern on the strip. Hold up the strip, and ask students if you have extended the pattern correctly.

Checking for Understanding

Make sure that students understand that a pattern repeats itself. Snap your fingers and clap your hands several times. Ask students to repeat the movements to extend the pattern.

Guided Practice

Give each student a pattern strip. Ask students to look at and identify the patterns that were started. Then direct them to continue the patterns by drawing, adding the shape cutouts, or stamping the objects on the strips. Walk around the classroom, and assist students as needed.

If you choose, have students use only shape cutouts to extend the patterns. That way, students can exchange strips with classmates so they can experience continuing a variety of patterns. Before students trade strips, walk by each desk to ensure students have continued the patterns correctly.

Closure

Have students trade their completed pattern strips with partners. Have students check to see that their partners correctly extended the patterns. If they did not, discuss how they should make corrections. Then ask students to draw one or two extended patterns in their math journals.

Independent Practice

Give each student a copy of the **Finish the Pattern reproducible (page 145).** Ask students to look at each pattern and then draw the correct shapes to extend it.

Name_____   Date_____

Finish the Pattern

Directions: Finish each pattern.

1.     ____ ____

2.    ____ ____

3.   ____ ____

4.   ____ ____ ____

5.    ____ ____ ____

6.   ____ ____ ____

Copyright © 2010 by David A. Sousa. All rights reserved. Reprinted from *Brain-Compatible Activities for Mathematics, Grades K–1*, by David A. Sousa. Thousand Oaks, CA: Corwin, www.corwinpress.com. Reproduction authorized only for the local school site or nonprofit organization that has purchased this book.

PATTERN NECKLACES

Objective

Students will create a patterned necklace.

Anticipatory Set

Prepare for the activity by dying batches of dried hollow pasta such as rigatoni and penne. Place some food coloring and rubbing alcohol in a large resealable plastic bag. Then place several pieces of dried pasta in the bag. Close the bag, and shake it until all the pasta is colored. Set the wet pasta on a newspaper to dry. Repeat this process to create other colors of pasta. Then cut several long pieces of yarn, one piece per student. Yarn pieces should be long enough to comfortably fit and hang low around a student's neck like a necklace. Tie one piece of dried pasta to one end of each yarn piece.

Read aloud the book *Lots and Lots of Zebra Stripes: Patterns in Nature* by Stephen R. Swinburne. Invite students to look at the photos and identify the patterns.

Purpose

Tell students that they will use dried pasta to create pattern necklaces.

Input

Remind students that patterns can be simple, such as AB AB, or more complex, such as AABC AABC. Reinforce the concept that patterns involve repetition.

Modeling

Model making an AB AB pattern with paperclips and crayons. Ask students if they can identify the pattern. Then continue by modeling several other simple patterns for students to identify. Ask them to tell you what comes next in the pattern.

Checking for Understanding

Check that students understand the concept of patterning. Ask them to give you a thumbs-up if they understand or a thumbs-down if they need more help.

Guided Practice

Give each student a length of the yarn that you prepared ahead of time with a piece of pasta tied to one end. Gather small groups of students together at separate tables. Place a pile of different-colored pasta in the center of each table that all group members can use.

Then invite students to string the pasta on their yarn pieces to make necklaces. Instruct them that each necklace must have a pattern. If you wish, give each group letter pattern cards (e.g., ABAB, ABCABC) to follow as they complete their necklaces. Encourage more proficient students to create more complex patterns.

Closure

Ask students to put on their necklaces and come to the front of the room, one group at a time. Invite the class to look at each group's necklaces and see if they can identify the pattern each student made. Have the class clap for each group as it shows its necklaces. Ask students to draw their necklaces in their math journals to record the patterns they made.

Independent Practice

Give each student crayons and a copy of the **Caterpillar Pattern reproducible (page 148).** Direct students to make patterns by coloring the caterpillars. Display students' completed reproducibles on a colorful bulletin board decorated like a garden. Title the bulletin board Our Pattern Garden.

Name_____ Date_____

Caterpillar Pattern

Directions: Color the caterpillar's body to make a pattern.

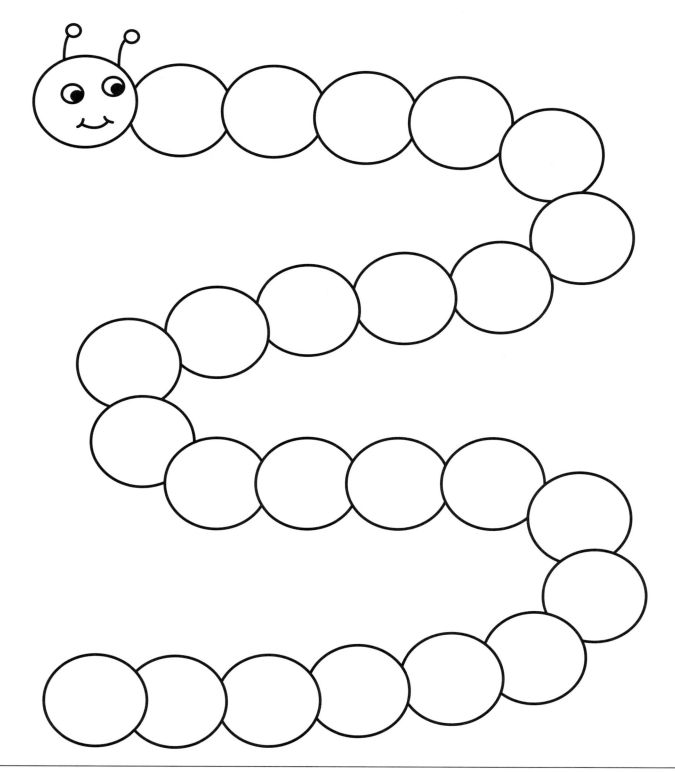

 Copyright © 2010 by David A. Sousa. All rights reserved. Reprinted from *Brain-Compatible Activities for Mathematics, Grades K–1*, by David A. Sousa. Thousand Oaks, CA: Corwin, www.corwinpress.com. Reproduction authorized only for the local school site or nonprofit organization that has purchased this book.

SORTING SHOES

Objective

Students will sort objects based on one attribute.

Anticipatory Set

Show students a pencil and a book. Give examples of how they are alike and how they are different. For example, "The pencil is round; the book is flat. You write with a pencil; you read a book." Then show students a pen. Ask, "Is the pen more like the pencil or the book? How are the pen and pencil alike?" (*They are both round. You use both to write.*)

Purpose

Tell students they will classify and sort objects.

Input

Explain to students that when they sort items, they are looking for all the ways the objects are alike.

Modeling

Show students a handful of buttons. Explain that you are going to sort the buttons into sets. Say, "I see that some buttons are blue, others are red, and some are white. I can sort the buttons by color and put all the blue ones together, all the red ones together, and all the white ones together." Then sort the buttons by color.

Afterward, tell students how you noticed that some buttons have two holes and some buttons have four holes. Explain how you can sort the buttons into two groups—those with two holes and those with four holes. Ask a volunteer to help you sort the buttons accordingly.

Checking for Understanding

Make sure students understand the concept of sorting. Draw three squares and two circles on the board. Ask students how they would sort these shapes. If they still have questions, provide further examples.

Guided Practice

Ask each student to take off one shoe. Ask one student to point out a shoe with shoelaces. Then ask another student to point out a shoe without shoelaces. Ask students how the shoes are alike and how they are different (e.g., one has laces and one does not have laces, one is small and one is large, one is white and one is blue).

Place the two different types of shoes in separate locations on the floor. Explain to students that they will be sorting their shoes based on one characteristic—laces or no laces. Then ask each student to place his or her shoe next to the shoe that is most similar (laces or no laces). As a group, examine each shoe, and decide whether it was placed in the correct group.

Closure

Ask students if there is another way that the shoes could be sorted. Tell them to work with partners to think of at least one other way to sort the shoes (e.g., by type, such as tennis shoes, boots, or sandals; by color; or by size). Then ask them to write or dictate in their math journals what they learned about sorting.

Independent Practice

Give each student a handful of different-sized and different-colored buttons. Have students sort the buttons into separate groups. Ask students to explain how they sorted their buttons (e.g., by shape, size, or color). Give more proficient students a larger number of buttons to sort. Or ask more proficient students to sort the buttons using two attributes (e.g., red, round buttons; blue, square buttons).

SORT AND CLASSIFY

Objective

Students will sort and classify objects based on one or two attributes.

Anticipatory Set

Show students the book *I Spy School Days* by Jean Marzollo. Turn to page 30, and show them the sorting and classifying pages. Discuss how the circles contain different categories of objects. Discuss the categories shown in each circle.

Purpose

Tell students that they will examine different objects and then place all the like objects into groups.

Input

Explain to students that when we want to classify objects into groups, we are looking for ways that the objects are the same and different. Objects that are the same should be sorted into the same groups. Point to a variety of classroom objects, such as a crayon, a pencil, a pen, and a marker. Ask students how all the objects are alike (*They are all used for drawing or writing.*).

Modeling

Ask several students to come to the front of the classroom. Tell the class, "I am going to find out how these students are alike and then sort them into like groups." Point out that some of the students have brown hair and some have blonde hair. Separate the students according to hair color. Then point out another way to sort the students. Explain that some are boys and some are girls. Separate the students into one group of girls and one group of boys. Point out that when we classify objects or people, we can often find many ways to sort them.

Checking for Understanding

Make sure students understand that they are looking for ways that objects are alike and different. Show students some pennies, nickels, and quarters. Ask students how they are alike (*They are round. They are all coins.*). Ask how they are different (*Some are brown; some are silver. They are different sizes.*).

Guided Practice

Show students four or five objects or attribute blocks that have only one different attribute. For example, the blocks can all be the same color and size but

> Teaching young students sorting and classifying skills enhances their number sense and their intuitive understandings about how to manipulate numbers.

have different shapes. Ask students to sort the blocks into different piles according to one likeness. If students don't classify the blocks by shape, place the objects back into a pile, and ask them to show another way they can be classified. As students become more proficient, add more objects, or use groups of objects that have several attributes. Then ask students to show several ways that the objects can be classified into groups.

Closure

Have students work with partners to classify a set of objects. Then ask them to discuss with each other how the items in each group are alike and how they are different. Ask students to record what they discovered in their math journals. They can write or dictate sentences or draw pictures to show how they classified the objects.

Independent Practice

Give each student a handful of candies in three colors and a sheet of construction paper with three large circles drawn on it. Direct students to classify the candy into three groups and place each group in a circle. Ask them to label each group with a name that describes how the candy is classified. After they are finished, invite students to tour the room and look at each other's papers to see how their classmates sorted and classified the candy.

6

Data Analysis and Probability

Ask Me a Question

Way to Vote!

Favorite Seasons

Roll and Record

Heads or Tails

Collect and Sort Data

Fun With Bar Graphs

Likely or Unlikely?

ASK ME A QUESTION

Objective

Students will ask a question and record the responses.

Anticipatory Set

Draw tally marks on the board while you count aloud. Point out that we can use a mark when counting. Each mark stands for one. Draw four tally marks, and say, "This stands for four—one, two, three, four." Ask students to count aloud with you.

Purpose

Tell students that they will ask questions and keep track of and record the answers.

Input

Brainstorm a list of yes-or-no questions with students. Explain that the questions should be able to be answered with only a yes or a no. Then go around the classroom asking each student if he or she has a pet at home. As students answer "yes" or "no," explain that this is a good example of a yes-or-no question. Then draw a simple T-chart on the board. Label the first column "Yes," and label the other column "No."

Modeling

Choose one question from the list you brainstormed with students. Ask a student that question. Then write his or her name in the appropriate column of the T-chart. Ask another student the same question, and write his or her name on the chart. Repeat the process until you have asked five or six students the question. Then show students that instead of writing names, you can simply draw a tally mark for each answer. Replace students' names with tally marks.

Discuss with students how sometimes we want to know who answered a question a certain way. In this situation, we would use names. But sometimes all we need to know is how many people answered yes or no. In this situation, we use tally marks to record the answers.

Checking for Understanding

Make sure students understand that they are choosing one question and asking it of different students. Ask students how they will keep track of the responses (*Write the students' names on the T-chart or make tally marks.*).

Guided Practice

Organize students into groups of five or six, and give each student a **Yes or No reproducible (page 156).** Have each student choose one question to ask the members of his or her group. Remind students to record the results on the reproducible. They can either write the name of each student or make a tally mark to show the answer.

Closure

Ask group members to discuss how many students answered yes and how many students answered no to their questions. Then have students write in their math journals about why it is important to record the information they collected.

Gather students back into a large group. Discuss what they learned during the activity. Ask them, "What else would you like to find out? How might you use what you learned today to find out other things about which you are curious?"

Independent Practice

Give students another copy of the Yes or No reproducible to take home. Help each student think of a yes-or-no question he or she would like to ask family members. Send home a short parent letter to accompany the reproducible so an older sibling or parent can help students complete the assignment. When students return to school the next day, invite them to share their questions and results with the rest of the class.

Name_____ Date_____

Yes or No

Directions: Ask six people a question. Record their answers on the chart.

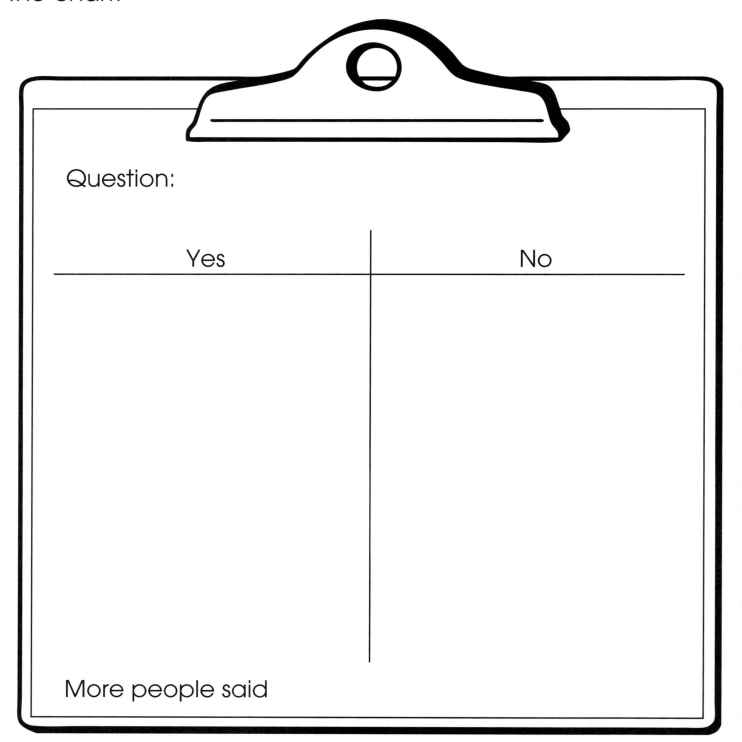

Question:

Yes	No

More people said

156 Copyright © 2010 by David A. Sousa. All rights reserved. Reprinted from *Brain-Compatible Activities for Mathematics, Grades K–1*, by David A. Sousa. Thousand Oaks, CA: Corwin, www.corwinpress.com. Reproduction authorized only for the local school site or nonprofit organization that has purchased this book.

WAY TO VOTE!

Objective

Students will create a concrete graph.

Anticipatory Set

Ask students if they have heard their parents talk about voting. Explain that many people vote to pick the president of the United States. Adults also vote on laws and rules. Tell them that children are not allowed to vote in true elections. You must be 18 to vote.

However, younger children might be able to vote on other things, such as what the family will watch on television, what they will eat for dinner, or where they will go on vacation. Ask students if they would like the opportunity to vote. Today they will get that chance!

Purpose

Tell students that they will vote on which book they would like read aloud to them. Explain that they will use Unifix cubes to show for which book they voted.

Input

Make a sign that reads, "Which book do you want read aloud?" Place the sign near two picture books. Explain to students that they will decide which of the two books they want to hear.

Modeling

Look at both books, and choose which one you want to read. Tell students that you will place your Unifix cube next to that book. When it is his or her turn to vote, each student should attach his or her Unifix cube to any cubes that are already placed next to the corresponding book. Show how to attach a cube to, or stack a cube on, the one you placed next to your book of choice.

Checking for Understanding

Make sure students understand that each student uses only one Unifix cube for his or her vote. Ask for a show of hands to ensure students know how to proceed with the vote.

Guided Practice

Hold up two picture books, and ask students which one they want read to them. Place each book on one side of your poster on a table or the chalk rail of the board. Give each student a Unifix cube, and invite him or her to place the cube next to the book that he or she wants read. Allow students to come to the front of the room, one at a time, to make their votes.

Afterward, point out the two stacks of cubes. Ask the class which book more students want read. Explain that they can use this same voting method to vote for other choices, such as which song they want to sing or which game they want to play.

Closure

Tell students to look at the two stacks of Unifix cubes. Ask, "Why is this method of voting easier than raising your hands and counting?" Allow students time to discuss the question and respond. Then ask, "Did you actually need to count the number of cubes to see which book got more votes? If not, how did you determine which book got more votes?"

Independent Practice

Divide the class into small student groups. Encourage each group to think of a question on which the class can vote (e.g., Which snack should the class share? Which class pet should we get? Which game should we play at recess? Which art project should we do this week?). Have group members write or dictate their question on a sheet of paper. When all groups are finished, collect all the papers.

Throughout the week, choose some of the questions for a student vote. Enlist students' help in coming up with other ideas (besides using Unifix cubes) for recording the votes. For example, students might draw tally marks or checkmarks, put different-colored chips in a bowl, or try a choral response.

FAVORITE SEASONS

Objective

Students will use pictures to create a class graph.

Anticipatory Set

Show students a set of simple instructions for a product, such as a game or a model airplane. Tell students that sometimes just written instructions are used and other times illustrations or diagrams are included. Ask students which instructions they think are easier to follow, those with pictures or those without pictures. Explain how visuals, or pictures, can make information easier to understand.

Purpose

Tell students they will create a graph showing the class's favorite season.

Input

Cut 3˝ × 3˝ squares from white paper. Create a class graph. Label the vertical axis "Number of Students." Label the horizontal axis "Season." Write the name of each season along the horizontal axis. Title the graph "What Is Your Favorite Season?" Show students your graph. Read the title aloud and ask, "What information will we be looking for when we work on this graph?" (*the number of people who like each of the four seasons*).

Modeling

Ask students to name the four seasons and what they like about each one. Tell them that you like summer best because in the summer the weather is warm and you can go swimming. Draw on a square of paper a swimming pool and a sun. Read the title of the graph aloud again, and then read the names of the seasons along the bottom of the graph. Explain that since you like summer best, you will place your square in that column. Model how to place your square in the appropriate column of the graph.

Checking for Understanding

Make sure students understand that they will be working together to create a class graph. The graph will show how many students like each of the seasons best. Remind students that they will choose only one of the four seasons.

Guided Practice

Give each student a white paper square. Ask each student to draw a picture of his or her favorite season. Explain that students can draw something that

Graphic organizers are valuable devices for improving understanding, meaning, and retention.

happens during that season (e.g., Valentine's Day in winter) or something that signifies the season (e.g., yellow, red, and orange leaves for autumn). Have each student write his or her name on the bottom of his or her square. Then give students pieces of tape, and ask them to place their squares in the corresponding columns for their favorite seasons.

After all students have taped their squares to the graph, review the graph with the whole class. Ask, "Which season did most students like the best? Which season did students like the least? How do you know?"

Closure

Ask students to identify the number of students who chose each season as their favorite. Have them determine the difference between the most-picked and the least-picked season. Ask questions to prompt thinking, such as, *How many more students like summer than fall?* and *How many fewer students like spring than winter?* Challenge students to think of strategies for answering the questions.

Invite students to reflect about the activity in their math journals. Provide them with a writing prompt, such as, *What did you learn about graphs?* or *Name one way that using a graph helps us to see information quickly.* Students can write or dictate their responses.

Independent Practice

Give each student a copy of the **Favorite Things reproducible (page 161).** Direct them to think of a question such as, *What is your favorite sport? What is your favorite flavor of ice cream? What is your favorite color?* or *What is your favorite animal?* Invite them to ask several students the question and then color in a box for each answer.

Name_____ Date_____

Favorite Things

Directions: Use this graph to record the answers to your question.

What is your favorite _____?

8		
7		
6		
5		
4		
3		
2		
1		

_____ _____ _____

Copyright © 2010 by David A. Sousa. All rights reserved. Reprinted from *Brain-Compatible Activities for Mathematics, Grades K–1*, by David A. Sousa. Thousand Oaks, CA: Corwin, www.corwinpress.com. Reproduction authorized only for the local school site or nonprofit organization that has purchased this book.

ROLL AND RECORD

Objectives

Students will compare different objects, try to roll the objects, and then decide if they are easy to roll.

Students will record their results on a chart.

Anticipatory Set

Ask students to raise their hands if they like apples. After they put down their hands, look confused and say, "I can't remember how many of you liked apples." Ask students who like apples to raise their hands again. This time, count how many people raised their hands, and write that number on the board or record those students' names. Explain how you recorded the information so you do not have to rely on remembering the number or the names. Now you have a record of your results.

Purpose

Tell students they will conduct a test to see whether an object can roll easily. They will then record their results on a graph.

Input

Show students several objects that they will be working with during the activity, such as a small rubber ball, a paper clip, a pencil, a marker, an empty thread spool, a block, and a small stuffed toy. Show students how to roll the ball gently across a table or your desk. Explain to students that they are not throwing the items; they should try to roll them gently.

Modeling

Show students the small rubber ball again, and roll it across the table. Tell them, "The ball rolled easily across the table." Draw a T-chart on the board. Title the first column "Things That Roll," and title the second column "Things That Do Not Roll." Draw a picture of the ball in the first column. Then try to roll the paper clip. Point out that it slides but it does not roll. Draw a picture of the paper clip in the second column.

Checking for Understanding

Make sure students understand that they should draw pictures of the objects they test in the appropriate columns of the chart.

Guided Practice

Divide the class into groups of three or four students. Give each group a copy of the **Roll It! reproducible (page 164)** and four or five objects (some that roll and some that do not roll). Ask one student in each group to roll an item. Then have students discuss whether the item rolled easily. Have another student in each group draw a picture of the item in the corresponding column of the chart on the reproducible.

You may wish to provide a greater number of objects for more proficient students to test. Or you may invite groups to switch objects with each other and repeat the experiment using another copy of the Roll It! reproducible.

Closure

Gather the class together as a large group. Hold up each object that was tested, one at a time. Ask students to show a thumbs-up if the object rolled easily and a thumbs-down if the object did not roll easily. If there is a disagreement among students, invite them to share their thoughts and repeat the experiment. Invite students to think of more objects that might roll and list them in their math journals (e.g., tire, cotton ball, can, crayon).

Independent Practice

Place more objects for students to test in the math center, along with a stack of blank T-charts. Students can work with partners to test objects for texture (smooth or rough), buoyancy (sink or float), or any other characteristic that is easily tested.

Name_____ Date_____

Roll It!

Things That Roll	Things That Do Not Roll

Copyright © 2010 by David A. Sousa. All rights reserved. Reprinted from *Brain-Compatible Activities for Mathematics, Grades K–1*, by David A. Sousa. Thousand Oaks, CA: Corwin, www.corwinpress.com. Reproduction authorized only for the local school site or nonprofit organization that has purchased this book.

HEADS OR TAILS

Objective

Students will toss a coin and record the number of times it lands on heads or tails.

Anticipatory Set

Show students some pictures of animals. Point out the head of an animal, and say, "This is the head." Point to the tail of the animal, and say, "This is the tail." Explain that a coin has a head and a tail too, but they are different from those of an animal. The top side of a coin is called "heads," and the bottom side of a coin is called "tails."

Purpose

Tell students they will be tossing a coin and keeping track of how many times it lands on heads and how many times it lands on tails.

Input

Show students a coin, and explain that one side has a face on it. Explain that this is the side we call "heads." Show the other side of the coin. Explain that each coin has a different picture on the bottom side, but we call this side "tails." If possible, use overhead coins on the overhead projector to show these heads and tails details to students.

Modeling

Draw a T-chart on the board. Title the left column "Heads" and the right column "Tails." Flip a coin in the air, and watch it land on the table. Tell students that the side that is faceup is the side you are looking at. Then identify which side the coin landed on, heads or tails. Draw a tally mark in the corresponding column of the T-chart.

Checking for Understanding

Make sure students understand which side of the coin is called "heads" and which is called "tails." Display one side of a coin, and ask students to identify it as heads or tails (or do this on the overhead with an overhead coin). Repeat several times with various coins, asking students to identify both sides.

Guided Practice

Organize students into pairs. Give each pair a coin and a piece of paper. While you demonstrate, direct pairs to fold their paper in half lengthwise and then unfold it. Tell them to write "Heads" at the top of the left side of their paper and "Tails" at the top of the right side.

Then have pairs flip their coin. Tell one student to flip the coin and identify which side lands faceup, heads or tails. Direct the other student to draw the tally mark in the appropriate column on the paper. After flipping the coin five times, have students switch roles and repeat the activity.

Closure

Ask students to discuss their results with the class. Point out that a coin has only two sides. It would make sense that the coin would land on heads the same number of times it would land on tails, but that doesn't usually happen. Ask students if any of them recorded equal results (the coin landed on heads the same number of times it landed on tails). Ask students to write about one thing they learned during this activity in their math journals. Invite them to reflect on why it is important to record results during an experiment.

Independent Practice

Tell students to draw six rows on a piece of paper and then label the rows using the numbers *1* through *6*. Tell students to roll a die and draw a tally mark in the row with the corresponding number. Have them repeat this several times and then discuss their results with a partner.

COLLECT AND SORT DATA

Objective

Students will use a tally chart to collect and sort data.

Anticipatory Set

Without saying anything, begin to write tally marks on the chalkboard. Stop when students are quiet or begin to question what you are doing. Ask them about the marks that they see. Find out if they are able to identify tally marks, and discuss why they may or may not use them.

Purpose

Tell students that they are going to learn about the importance of recording data on a tally chart.

Input

Tell students that tally charts are helpful for keeping track of counting. Give two examples: during elections (for counting votes) and during contests (for keeping track of points). Teach students the term *data* by explaining that it is information that someone has collected. One way that data can be recorded and organized is on a *tally chart*. Explain that "a tally chart contains tally marks: these marks represent numbers." Use tally marks on the board to represent the numbers *4*, *7*, and *18*.

Modeling

Draw the following chart on the board:

Ice Cream	|||
Cake	||
Cookies	ꟼꜲ
Candy	ꟼꜲ |||

Using a show of hands, model how to use tally marks to record the information about students' preferences. Think aloud as you record the responses: "Jayden, do you like ice cream, cake, cookies, or candy best? She likes candy, so I'll put one tally mark next to candy."

Pose questions about the information you have recorded. Have students help you count the tally marks and record the final numbers. If appropriate, help students make comparisons using data. "Do more people like cake or candy?"

Allow students to practice writing tally marks on the board. Show them how to indicate the number *five,* using four marks with a fifth tally line across the other four.

Checking for Understanding

Ask students to raise their right hands if they understand or their left hands if they need more explanation.

Guided Practice

Guided practice helps eliminate initial errors and alerts students to the critical steps in applying new skills.

Distribute a copy of the **Totally Teeth Tally Chart reproducible (page 169)** to each student. Tell students that as a class, they are going to complete the tally chart. Guide students in a step-by-step manner, collecting data about how many teeth students have lost. Guide students in recording their tally marks for each number of teeth lost. Count, compare, and discuss the information recorded.

Independent Practice

Using their **Tally Chart reproducibles (page 170),** tell students to write a list of items they can count (books, pencils, people with red shirts, names that start with the letter *s*). Next to each item in the list, show tally marks to count how many there are of each item.

Closure

Invite students to respond to the journal prompts on page 179.

Name_____ Date_____

Totally Teeth Tally Chart

Directions: How many teeth have your classmates lost? Listen to your teacher for directions about how to record the numbers and tally marks in the chart.

Number of Teeth	Tally Marks	Total

Copyright © 2010 by David A. Sousa. All rights reserved. Reprinted from *Brain-Compatible Activities for Mathematics, Grades K–1*, by David A. Sousa. Thousand Oaks, CA: Corwin, www.corwinpress.com. Reproduction authorized only for the local school site or nonprofit organization that has purchased this book.

Tally Chart

Directions: Write what you will count in the first column. Tally how many. Count the tally marks and write the number in the last column.

Item	Tally Marks	Total Number

Copyright © 2010 by David A. Sousa. All rights reserved. Reprinted from *Brain-Compatible Activities for Mathematics, Grades K–1*, by David A. Sousa. Thousand Oaks, CA: Corwin, www.corwinpress.com. Reproduction authorized only for the local school site or nonprofit organization that has purchased this book.

FUN WITH BAR GRAPHS

Objective

Students will construct a bar graph to show data.

Anticipatory Set

Display a large bag of colored candies such as Skittles or M&Ms. Tell students that you want to know how many of each color are inside. Empty the bag, and ask volunteers to help you sort the candies by color. Count and record the amounts, using tally marks on the board.

Purpose

Tell students that they are going to learn how to organize data using various bar graphs.

Input

Before the activity, display several pictures of bar graphs. Your math textbook and the Web are good sources for samples. Point out the bars, and explain how the bars represent numbers for each item. Encourage students to talk about bar graphs they have seen or used. Talk about how data are used to construct a bar graph and the ways we use bar graphs to easily interpret data. Think aloud while drawing conclusions about the sample graphs you selected: "I can see from this graph that more people buy apples than avocados at the market."

Modeling

Using the data from the Anticipatory Set, model how to construct a bar graph on the board or on chart paper. Enlarge the **Colored Candy Bar Graph reproducible (page 173).** Model how to transfer data from the tally chart to the bar graph. Create a bar for each color, and extend it equivalent to the number of candies. Color each bar with the correct color.

Think aloud as you interpret the results of the graph: "There are more green candies than purple candies. But there are fewer purple candies than red candies."

Checking for Understanding

Use a thumbs-up or thumbs-down technique to check for understanding.

Guided Practice

Distribute copies of the **Perfect Pet Bar Graph reproducible (page 174).** Tell students that you will guide them through constructing a bar graph. Write the names of five kinds of pets on the board. Ask each student which kind

Stay within the capacity limits for working memory of the students' age group.

of pet makes the perfect pet. Record students' responses using tally marks, and prompt them to record the information on their own reproducibles. Guide them to fill in the missing information. Initiate a discussion about the results. If appropriate, ask students to perform calculations to compare data: "How many more students prefer fish to hamsters?"

Ask volunteers to count the tally marks and jot down the answers. Then have students write the first pet name on the bar graph. Instruct students to use their fingers to trace over to the number for that pet and then color the graph: "Put your finger on the word *hamster.* How many people think hamsters are the perfect pet? Four. OK, move your finger over until it is on the number *four.* Now use a crayon to color the four boxes."

Closure

Invite students to respond to the math journal prompts on page 179.

Colored Candy Bar Graph

Colors of Candies	Tally Marks	Total

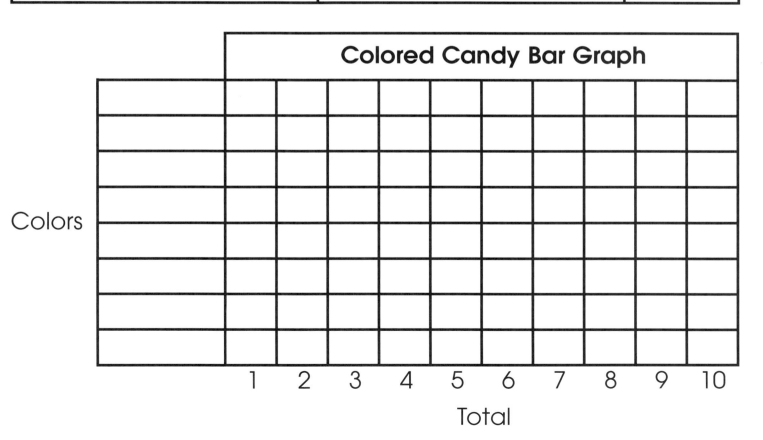

Colored Candy Bar Graph

Colors

1 2 3 4 5 6 7 8 9 10

Total

Copyright © 2010 by David A. Sousa. All rights reserved. Reprinted from *Brain-Compatible Activities for Mathematics, Grades K–1*, by David A. Sousa. Thousand Oaks, CA: Corwin, www.corwinpress.com. Reproduction authorized only for the local school site or nonprofit organization that has purchased this book.

173

Name_____ **Date**_____

Perfect Pet Bar Graph

Directions: Complete the bar graph using the information you collected.

Pets	Tally Marks	Total

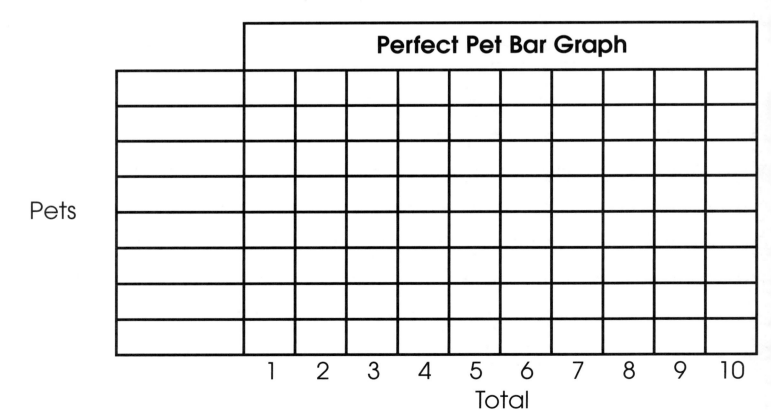

174 Copyright © 2010 by David A. Sousa. All rights reserved. Reprinted from *Brain-Compatible Activities for Mathematics, Grades K–1*, by David A. Sousa. Thousand Oaks, CA: Corwin, www.corwinpress.com. Reproduction authorized only for the local school site or nonprofit organization that has purchased this book.

LIKELY OR UNLIKELY?

Objective

Students will identify events as likely or unlikely.

Anticipatory Set

Read aloud *Pinkalicious* by Elizabeth Kann. When you are finished, ask students if they think the story could really happen. Have them give reasons why or why not.

Purpose

Tell students that they will work with groups to identify events that are likely and unlikely to occur.

Input

Ask students to identify situations in their daily lives that are likely to happen (*We will eat dinner tonight.*). Then discuss events that are unlikely to happen (*All my hair will fall out tonight.*). Talk about how data can help us determine if something is likely or unlikely to happen. For example, if 12 of my classmates have the flu, it is likely I will get the flu too. In the month of April, the temperature has risen each week. It is likely the temperature will continue to rise.

> Information is most likely to get stored if it makes sense and has meaning.

Modeling

Start by writing a sentence about an event that is unlikely: "All students will wear pink shoes tomorrow." Then do a quick illustration of the scenario. Finally, show the picture, read the sentence, and explain why the event is unlikely. Repeat the process with an event that is likely to occur.

Checking for Understanding

Make sure the teams understand the difference between an event that is likely to happen and an event that is unlikely to happen. Invite volunteers to give examples to demonstrate understanding.

Guided Practice

Divide the class into two groups. Tell one group that it is Team Likely, and tell the other group that it is Team Unlikely. Provide them with sentence strips and drawing paper. Tell team members that they are going to work together to draw or write examples of events that are likely to occur (if they are on Team Likely) or unlikely to occur (if they are on Team Unlikely).

Write the following sentences on the board.

Students will learn math.

The school will melt.

Students will play at recess.

The principal will fly above the school.

Students will eat lunch.

Teachers will fall asleep in class.

Teams must first identify whether each event is likely or unlikely to occur in school this week. Then they will draw a picture of the event and write a sentence.

Explain to the teams that they will be given a time limit to complete their work. At the end of this time limit, teams will present their pictures and sentence strips. Make sure students use correct terms when describing events as likely and unlikely. It is also important for students to provide a rationale for deciding whether the event is likely or unlikely. For each complete and correct idea, teams earn a point. Tally the points on the board. The team with the most points at the end of the game will win.

Closure

Invite Team Likely to the front of the classroom. Ask each team member to read one sentence strip or describe one picture. Invite Team Unlikely to the front of the classroom. Ask each of its team members to read one sentence strip or describe one picture.

Tell all team members to return to their desks and take a minute to reflect on what they learned today. Then tell students to describe or illustrate a funny likely or unlikely event in their math journals. Encourage them to make a connection between the terms they learned and real life.

Independent Practice

Attaching a positive emotion to the mathematics lesson helps the students to see mathematics as having real-life applications.

Give each student a copy of the **Likely or Unlikely? reproducible (page 177)** to complete individually. Explain that students will circle the events that are likely to happen next week and place an X over the events that are unlikely to happen next week.

Name_____ Date_____

Likely or Unlikely?

Directions: Circle things that are likely to happen. Put an X on things that are unlikely to happen.

An owl will be your teacher.

You will have homework.

It will rain.

You will play with your friends.

You will eat breakfast.

A bunny will learn to read.

Copyright © 2010 by David A. Sousa. All rights reserved. Reprinted from *Brain-Compatible Activities for Mathematics, Grades K–1*, by David A. Sousa. Thousand Oaks, CA: Corwin, www.corwinpress.com. Reproduction authorized only for the local school site or nonprofit organization that has purchased this book.

Name_____   Date_____

Journal Page

Today I learned

This adds to what I already know about

What I learned today can help me

Copyright © 2010 by David A. Sousa. All rights reserved. Reprinted from *Brain-Compatible Activities for Mathematics, Grades K–1*, by David A. Sousa. Thousand Oaks, CA: Corwin, www.corwinpress.com. Reproduction authorized only for the local school site or nonprofit organization that has purchased this book.

Answer Key

Counting Objects (page 8)

A. 3

B. 5

C. 6

D. 4

E. 7

F. 2

More or Less (page 16)

A. Answers will vary. Drawing should show 6 or more items.

B. Answers will vary. Drawing should show 5 or more items.

C. Answers will vary. Drawing should show 4 or fewer items.

D. Answers will vary. Drawing should show 1 or 2 items.

Greater Than, Less Than (page 22)

A. 33 > 4

B. 52 > 19

C. 66 < 93

D. 21 < 81

E. 25 < 27

F. 71 > 10

G. 46 < 51

H. 60 > 17

I. 90 < 92

J. 65 < 77

K. 42 > 29

L. 16 < 58

Twos, Fives, and Tens (page 28)

A. 2, 4, 6, 8, 10, 12, 14, 16, 18, 20, 22, 24, 26, 28, 30, 32, 34, 36, 38, 40

B. 5, 10, 15, 20, 25, 30, 35, 40, 45, 50, 55, 60, 65, 70, 75, 80, 85, 90, 95, 100

C. 10, 20, 30, 40, 50, 60, 70, 80, 90, 100

Add the Sets (page 32)

A. 5 stars

B. 5 triangles

C. 6 diamonds

D. 3 hearts

E. 6 ovals

F. 4 squares

Ready, Set . . . Add! (page 49)

A. 3

B. 7

C. 5

D. 9

E. 11

F. 11

G. 12

H. 8

I. 10

J. 11

Counting Sides (page 75)

Answers will vary. Possible responses include:

0 sides—circles, ovals

3 sides—triangles

4 sides—squares, rectangles, trapezoids, rhombuses, diamonds

The Same Shape (page 87)

Answers will vary. Possible responses include:

Circle—cookie, clock, ball

Square—cracker, box, window

Triangle—ice cream cone, party hat, flag

Rectangle—book, table, lunch bag

Smart Shape Riddles (page 94)

1. triangle
2. sphere
3. square

Clock Shop Practice (page 130)

A. 5:00

B. 2:30

C. 8:30

D. 10:00

Number Patterns (page 140)

A. 6, 7, 8

B. 1, 2, 1

C. 4, 3, 2

D. 8, 10, 12

E. 9, 10, 11

F. 1, 2, 3

G. 4, 2, 0

H. 2, 5, 5

Finish the Pattern (page 145)

1. star, heart
2. circle, triangle
3. triangle, heart, heart
4. square, circle, diamond
5. star, star, happy face
6. heart, triangle, oval

Likely or Unlikely? (page 177)

Circled answers will vary but may include:

> You will have homework.
> It will rain.
> You will play with your friends.
> You will eat breakfast.

Crossed out answers will vary but should include:

> An owl will be your teacher.
> A bunny will learn to read.

References

Emberley, E. (2001). *The wing of a flea.* New York: Little, Brown.

Harding, D. (2003). *Math graphic organizers: Simple and effective strategies for solving math word problems.* Huntington Beach, CA: Creative Teaching Press.

Hoban, T. (2000). *Cubes, cones, cylinders, and spheres.* New York: Greenwillow.

Marzollo, J. (1995). *I spy school days.* New York: Cartwheel.

National Council of Teachers of Mathematics. (2005). *Principles and standards for school mathematics.* Reston, VA: Author.

National Council of Teachers of Mathematics. (2008). *Curriculum focal points for prekindergarten through grade 8 mathematics: Kindergarten.* Retrieved December 18, 2007, from http://www.nctm.org/standards/focalpoints.aspx?id=330&ekmensel=c580fa7b_10_52_330_5

Sousa, D. A. (2006). *How the brain learns* (3rd ed.). Thousand Oaks, CA: Corwin.

Sousa, D. A. (2008). *How the brain learns mathematics.* Thousand Oaks, CA: Corwin.

Swinburne, S. (2002). *Lots and lots of zebra stripes: Patterns in nature.* Honesdale, PA: Boyds Mills Press.

TERC. (n.d.). *Investigations in number, data, and space: Kindergarten math content: Number and operations: Whole numbers.* Retrieved December 12, 2007, from http://investigations.terc.edu/library/curric-gl/math_content_gk_2ed.pdf

CORWIN
A SAGE Company

The Corwin logo—a raven striding across an open book—represents the union of courage and learning. Corwin is committed to improving education for all learners by publishing books and other professional development resources for those serving the field of PreK–12 education. By providing practical, hands-on materials, Corwin continues to carry out the promise of its motto: **"Helping Educators Do Their Work Better."**